THE MANAGEMENT OF CONSTRUCTION PROJECTS

CASE STUDIES FROM THE USA AND UK

Herb Nahapiet
French Kier
Construction Managemei

Janine Nahapiet
Templeton College
The Oxford Centre for
Management Studies

ii

Nahapiet, H.
  The management of construction projects: case studies from the USA and UK.
  1. Industrial project management – Case studies I. Title   II. Nahapiet, J.
  658.4'04'0722   HD69.P75

  ISBN 0–906600–75–8

Published by The Chartered Institute of Building, February 1985.

CONTENTS

PREFACE

There have been a number of reports which have compared the performance of the UK and US construction industries. This report is definitely not an attempt to dig up the roots all over again; it looks beyond the straight comparison of performance and examines the managerial and organizational aspects of projects. Hence, quite intentionally, there is no detailed discussion on the problems of making international comparisons caused by such things as fluctuations in exchange rates and differences in culture and attitudes.

The co-authors, Janine Nahapiet with her background as a Fellow at Templeton College, Oxford and in depth knowledge of organizational theory, and Herb Nahapiet with his experience and knowledge as a construction project manager, make them eminently suitable to write such a report. This blend of knowledge and experience comes through in the report which is easy to read and contains a wealth of knowledge.

There is no single best approach to buying building work. Clients want projects to be built on time and within budget with the minimum risk exposure. The most appropriate form of contractual arrangement will be selected to suit the particular requirements of the project. Very little thought is usually given to the impact that the contractual arrangement has on the organizational framework by which the project will be built.

It is people who build buildings. The way the communicate, organize themselves, and are managed is just as important as getting the design correct. One can be just as creative about management as design.

The report doesn't set out to say the UK builds slower or faster than US; it doesn't attempt to analyse costs in detail, nor does it say, 'these are the lessons we must learn from the USA'. It uses a case study approach to investigate areas that hitherto have not been considered in detail.

It makes a valuable contribution to our knowledge of the subject area. Hopefully, clients and members of the construction industry will give serious thought to the contents of this report.

Roger Flanagan.

FOREWORD

The study described in this report was carried out under the auspices of The Chartered Institute of Building, Queen Elizabeth II Silver Jubilee Scholarship Fund. We gratefully acknowledge the financial support given by the CIOB, French Kier Construction and Templeton College, The Oxford Centre for Management Studies.

We are also grateful to the many people and organisations in the USA and the UK who have given generously of their knowledge, time and experience. In some cases they have wished to remain anonymous for personal, professional or commercial reasons. Where possible they have been included in the acknowledgements. In particular, we wish to thank Dr. Roger Flanagan of Reading University for his advice and support throughout the study.

The views expressed in the report are our own and are not necessarily those of the Institute nor of our employers.

1. Introduction and summary of findings

INTRODUCTION

1.1 The last few years have been an especially difficult period for the UK construction industry. Construction output has fallen steadily, partly as a result of the recession but also because of the uncertainties generated by some projects exceeding their time and cost budgets. At a time when the costs of building and of borrowing money are regarded as high, clients are less willing or able to tolerate such uncertainties.

1.2 Concern about this state of affairs has stimulated several reviews of the industry and led to a series of reports which have identified potential areas for change[1]*. These include design and contract procedures, the organisation of design and construction, construction methods, and the client's responsibility in the building process.

1.3 The importance of these factors, and the underlying concern about the industry, have been further emphasised by the findings of international comparisons of building performance. For example, studies have shown that the performance of US construction is better in terms of speed and cost of construction than that of the UK or, indeed, some continental European countries[2]. Clearly, there are many variables which might explain these differences, not least cultural factors, different industry structures and working practices. However, there is much to suggest that the different types of contract used in the USA, along with differences in organisation and in planning and control procedures, may also explain variations in the efficiency and effectiveness of project delivery.

1.4 The research to date has drawn attention to the issues and highlighted some major influences on project performance. However, important gaps remain in what is known. For example, there is still relatively little information describing the managerial aspects of project delivery. Even more significant, although several surveys have explored the impact of particular variables across a number of projects, there have been relatively few which have analysed a wider range of technical, contractual, managerial and organisational factors involved in any one project. The study described in this report has been undertaken to add to existing knowledge of these aspects. It has been stimulated by the desire to develop a greater understanding of the inter- relationships between these factors and the ways in which they together may influence project performance.

OBJECTIVES OF THE STUDY

1.5 The main goal of the study was:

- **to describe and analyse current practice in building construction, with particular reference to the managerial and organisational aspects of projects.**

1.6 In the light of recent research, it was considered that it would be instructive to examine these aspects by looking at projects both in the United States and the United Kingdom. The primary aim in so doing was not to undertake a further comparison of US and UK construction performance but rather to provide different settings in which to explore the management of projects and the possible influences on performance. Thus, the particular objectives for the study were specified as follows:

- **to describe and compare the project delivery process in the USA and UK with respect to the following features:**
  - **the ways in which the various parties are organised, especially at the interfaces between them; this includes contractual arrangements;**

References are given at the end of each chapter.

> — the management of projects with respect to planning, programming, co-ordination and
>   control procedures;
> — construction methods.

- to obtain the view of those prominent in the industry about the influences on project
  performance.

SCOPE OF THE STUDY
1.7   A case study approach
The starting point for the study was the assumption that project performance is a function of the
interaction between the set of human, technical, organisational and environmental factors involved in
any one project[3]. Although the managerial and organisational aspects of projects were of particular
interest, it was considered important to examine these in relation to other project characteristics, such
as client attributes and requirements, site characteristics, and construction methods. Thus rather than
examining a narrower set of factors across a large sample, a relatively detailed study of a small number
of building projects was undertaken[4].
Ten building projects were examined and these are listed in Table 1.1[5]. There are six US projects
which range in value from £1.3 million to £19.4 million. They include three office blocks, two
manufacturing facilities and one warehouse. The four UK projects are all office blocks and range in
value from £2.5 million to £11 million[6]. Full details of the case studies are given in the Appendix.

1.8   Data collection
Semi-structured interviews, questionnaires, project documentation and visits to each of the sites were
used to gather the following information for each case study:

   i.   the role of the client on the project, especially in relation to the type of contract to be used;
  ii.   the characteristics of the building, its location and the construction process;
 iii.   the managerial and technical aspects of planning and programming at design, bid and construc-
      tion phases;
 iv.   the ways in which the various parties were organised, especially at the interfaces between the
      several groups involved at each stage of the project;
  v.   the levels of performance achieved, in terms of the speed and cost of project delivery.

In addition, given the interest in the opinions of those active in the industry about the influences
on project performance, interviews were also used to ask broader questions about such topics as:

   i.   The factors influencing the speed and cost of construction;
  ii.   the criteria for choosing between different forms of contractual arrangements[7].

In all, eighty people were interviewed in the course of the study. Although most of these were directly
involved with the selected projects, the sample also includes several other people with acknowledged
expertise and experience in building construction. (Details of the individuals and organisations who
participated are given in the Acknowledgements).

STRUCTURE OF THE REPORT
1.9   The findings of the study have been presented in four main chapters which deal with the
following subjects: contractual arrangements, the management of design and construction,
construction methods and the vexed question of project performance. The final chapter draws
together the main conclusions and discusses the implications of the study for future practice and
research. The Appendix contains a case history for each of the projects.
The chapters have been written so that they are self-contained and can be read separately, according

Table 1.1 Description, main features and location of projects

Case study no.	Description of project and location	Project* cost	Pre-construction time (months)	Construction time (months)	Completion date	Contractual arrangement
US PROJECTS						
US1	Corporate offices (Alabama)	$42m	8	30	Oct '81	Lump sum
US2	Manufacturing facility (Georgia)	$2.3m	6	7	June '80	Construction management
US3	Corporate offices (Utah)	$29m	3	33	Feb '82	Construction management
US4	Warehouse (California)	$34.8m	3	23	Sept '82	Construction management
US5	Expansion of existing manufacturing facilities (California)	$22m	3	8	Sept '82	Design build
US6	Speculative offices (Massachusetts)	$14.4m	n/a	16	June '81	Negotiated (GMP)
UK PROJECTS						
UK1	Speculative shops and offices (London)	£8.7m	n/a	31	June '81	Two-stage negotiated
UK2	Speculative offices (Buckinghamshire)	£2.9m	3	18	March '81	Negotiated
UK3	Speculative offices (Hampshire)	£8.2m	8	18	Nov '82	Management contracting
UK4	Corporate offices (London)	£10.9m	n/a	25	Dec '81	Two stage negotiated

KEY
n/a = not available
GMP = guaranteed maximum price

*The currency exchange rate at the time was $1.8 = £1.00

to the interest of readers. So as to enable users of the report to select the material of most relevance, a summary of each of the chapters is given below.

SUMMARY OF FINDINGS
1.10   Contractual arrangements

- Contract selection is important because contracts establish the overall organisational framework within which project delivery takes place.
- Those interviewed believe that different contractual arrangements offer different costs and benefits to clients.
  a. Lump sum contracts were regarded as creating relatively simple, clear relationships which offer the client price security. At the same time, they were thought to lead to slower and possibly more costly project delivery and to be prone to conflict where circumstances require flexibility and change.
  b. By incorporating more construction expertise into the design process and offering scope for fast tracking, negotiated contracts were seen as enabling faster project delivery. At the same time, they were thought to offer less price certainty than lump sum contracts and to create some confusion over roles and responsibilities.
  c. Construction management contracts and management contracting were regarded as facilitating project delivery to tight time and cost schedules; they were seen as establishing more flexible relationships between those involved in all stages of the project and giving the client better information and advice as a basis for decisions. At the same time, some considered that they offer clients relatively little price security while adding another fee and a further organisational interface to be managed.
  d. Design-build contracts were viewed as simplifying communication and co-ordination between all those involved in a project and offering flexibility in the approach adopted at each stage. However, they were thought to place less emphasis on design quality, to make value for money difficult to assess and to run the risk of reduced client control of the project.
- In the sample of cases three factors were related to contract usage:
  a. The lump sum and negotiated contracts were used only by primary constructors or experienced clients; inexperienced clients used management contracting.
  b. Non-traditional contractual arrangements were used on all those projects for which the performance requirements were regarded as particularly demanding.
  c. Where demanding project performance was associated with construction complexity, clients deliberately selected contractual arrangements which reduced the number of organisations involved and which simplified communication across key project interfaces.
- The study suggests that no one form of contract is universally the best. Rather, the appropriate contractual arrangement varies according to the type of client, his time and cost requirements and the characteristics of the project.*

1.11   The Management of design and construction

- Project management processes fall into two broad types: formal systems, such as planning and programming, and personal contacts, including client representatives and meetings.
- During the preconstruction period, the form of programming adopted varied across the sample of cases. In the USA, bar charts or network analysis were used. In the UK, milestone dates or bar charts were employed.
- Similarly, during the construction period, the form of programming also varied between projects. Network analysis predominated in the USA whereas in the UK bar charts were used.

---

* See also FRANKS, J. *Building procurement systems*, 1984. CIOB.

- The more sophisticated planning methods were used on those projects which were characterised by relatively high performance requirements.
- Network analysis seemed to be used primarily as a guide to understand the dependencies of all the design and construction activities across the whole project rather than as a scheduling tool.
- Those cases which produced the greatest number of reports and documentation were located in the USA and were managed by construction management contracts.
- No clear relationship was found between the method of client representation and other project features such as client requirements, contractual arrangements or project performance.
- There seems to be a a greater overall investment in project management in the USA than UK, regardless of contractual arrangements adopted. This is particularly striking in respect of meetings but can also be seen across other formal and personal procedures for project management.

1.12   Construction methods

- The US urban sites were less congested than their counterparts in the UK, thereby allowing the contractor more freedom to construct more easily.
- In the USA, simplicity seemed to be the overriding rule in the form and detail of the structure, e.g. reinforced concrete frame design in the USA regularly allows 'flying formwork', larger concrete pours, the elimination of 'kickers' and short minimum striking times for falsework, the combination of which leads to ease of construction and much faster construction times.
- Planning restrictions and ground conditions in the UK limit the height of buildings more than in the USA, so that more economical and speedy structural frame construction is often excluded.
- In the UK design does not generally appear to be as clearly oriented towards construction, methods. However, where construction requirements have been taken into account the cases show that ease of construction has resulted.
- There is a comparative lack of external scaffolding on US construction sites.
- In all US cases there were no 'wet' trades, whereas they were common-place on the UK cases.
- In the US cases the design of elements normally associated with the finishing trades also leads to ease of construction.

1.13   The vexed question of project performance

- The majority of US buildings were constructed faster than those in the UK.
- The factors identified as significant influences by those involved in faster projects were: the knowledge and experience of the client, contractual arrangements, good working relationships between the main parties and simplification and standardisation of construction.
- Those jobs which were constructed quickly were all ones in which the client made a substantial investment in project management.
- The difference between the performance of US and UK projects is not so marked on cost as it is on speed, although for the three most similar buildings, the costs of construction were significantly less in the USA than in the UK.
- Two factors were identified by interviewees as contributing to good performance on the low cost projects. These were contractual arrangments and the simplicity and standardisation of design.
- Project success is a subjective as well as objective assessment. Notwithstanding variations between the projects examined, in terms of the speed, cost and quality levels attained, most of the cases were regarded by those involved as being relatively successful.

1.14   Reflections and future directions

- The project delivery process is best understood as a set of highly interdependent activities; project performance is a function of the interaction between the human, technical, organisational and managerial factors involved in a project and the ways in which these relate to client attributes and requirements and wider environmental factors.
- The study emphasises the need for clients to develop clear objectives, to select contractual arrangements in the light of their in-house experience and ability in managing projects, and to sustain a high level of involvement throughout all stages of a project.
- The trend towards diversification of project management approaches is likely to continue. As a result, an important skill for those involved in the industry is the ability to match the various approaches to the particular requirements of clients and their projects. Also of increasing importance is the ability to work in new patterns of relationship with other parties in the industry.
- There is much to be learned from studying projects, from their inception through to completion. Further research is needed to increase understanding of the needs of clients, interface management, the role of formal planning systems in project management and building design and construction methods.

References

1 These reports include:
  NEDO. (1975). The public client and the construction industries. London: HMSO.
  NEDO. (1976). The professions in the construction industry. London: HMSO.
  NEDO. (1978). Construction for industrial recovery. London: HMSO.
2 These studies include:
  NEDO. (1976). Working party on engineering construction performance. London: HMSO.
  SLOUGH ESTATES LIMITED. (1976 & 1976). Industrial investment: a case study in factory building.
  DEPARTMENT OF CONSTRUCTION MANAGEMENT, UNIVERSITY OF READING. (1979). UK and US construction industries: a comparison of design and contract procedures. London: Royal Institution of Chartered Surveyors.
  CONSTRADO. (1981). Design and construction methods for multi-storey office buildings in North America. Croydon: Constructional Steel Research and Development Organisation.
  FREEMAN, I.L. (1981). Comparative studies of the construction industries in Great Britain and North America: a review. Watford: Building Research Establishment.
  CIRIA. (1983). Management contracting. London: Construction Industry Research and Information Association.
  NEDO. (1983). Faster building for industry. London: HMSO.
3 This assumption reflects a systems perspective. The main features of the systems approach and their relevance to the construction industry are discussed in the following:
  HIGGIN, G. and JESSOP, N. (1965). Communications in the building industry. London: Tavistock.
  MORRIS, P.W.G. (1972). A study of selected building projects in the context of theories of organisation. Ph.D. Thesis, University of Manchester.
  MORRIS, P.W.G. (1974). Systems study of project management. *Building* January and February.
  NAHAPIET, H.N. and NAHAPIET, J. E. (1982). Project characteristics, contractual arrangements and the organisation of construction. Working Paper of the Oxford Centre for Management Studies.
  CLELAND, D.I. and KING, W.R. (1983). Systems analysis and project management. Tokyo: McGraw-Hill.
4 Whilst recognising that a case study approach would preclude statistical analysis and interpretation of the data, a sample of projects was sought which would be similar enough to permit reasonable comparison. The procedure for project selection was as follows:
  a.   People were contacted in the United States who were known to be actively involved in the construction industry and interested in the subject matter of the research. Through them access was sought to study

medium-sized projects involving the construction of industrial or commercial facilities. They were selected for the following reasons:

    i.   they represent an important building sector;
    ii. they avoid extremes of project simplicity and complexity;
    iii. they are managed by a wide range of contractual arrangements.

Wherever possible, projects were to be either approaching completion or only just finished on site so that key project personnel could be contacted. Finally, given the interest in contractual relationships, a sample was sought which included projects managed though the major forms of contract available but which was especially representative of the newer forms of contractual arrangement.

The US fieldwork was done in one continuous period of seven weeks finishing in September 1981. The projects differed from the criteria listed because those who wished to be involved in the study were unable to provide projects which matched the specification;

  b. On return to England, access to projects similar to those studied in the United States was sought. The UK projects were studied intermittently over a period of several months during the Spring and Summer of 1982. This is because of the time taken to identify and secure access to appropriate projects and the need to arrange interviews etc. at times which did not disrupt other work commitments.

5 In fact, 13 projects were investigated. Four US cases were excluded from the detailed analysis for the following reasons:

  a. one was a civil engineering project falling outside the stated concern with building projects;
  b. one of the projects had been completed several months before the visit. Although there was a valuable discussion with the client, it was not possible to contact and meet all the relevant parties or obtain full project details;
  c. on of the projects had not yet started on site. Once again, it was not possible to collect full project details.

6 The sample includes more US than UK cases because of the difficulty in gaining access to suitable UK projects.

7 The study can thus be regarded as combining the two approaches defined by Freeman (1981) as 'data-based' and 'opinion-based'.

FREEMAN, I.L. (1981). Comparative studies of the construction industries in Great Britain and North America: a review, Watford: Building Research Establishment.

2. Contractual arrangements

INTRODUCTION

2.1 One of the prime aims of the study was to explore different forms of contractual arrangement for construction project delivery. Of special interest were the reasons why different forms of contract were selected by clients and what clients, together with those in the industry, believe to be their relative strengths and weaknesses. Although there are many different forms of contract available these can be regarded as falling into a number of distinguishable types[1]. The sample of cases to be studied was deliberately constructed so as to include several different contractual types and to be representative of the contractual arrangements which currently predominate in the industry. These were: lump sum contracts and their modified version, the negotiated contract, construction management, management contracting and design-build. The distribution of the sample of cases in respect of these arrangements is given in Table 2.1.

Table 2.1   Distribution of contractual arrangements obtained in sample

	Case study numbers		
Type of contract	US	UK	Total number
1 Lump sum	1		1
2 Negotiated contract	6	1,2,4	4
3 Construction management	2,3,4		3
4 Management contract		3	1
5 Design-build	5		1

2.2 This chapter falls into four main sections. Firstly, the reasons why contract selection is an important element of construction project management are reviewed. This is followed by a general analysis of the distinguishing features of the main alternative contractual arrangements. In the third section, the case studies and the light they throw on contractual arrangements are examined. Finally, by linking the findings of this study to other works, it is suggested that there may not be one 'best' form of contract but that which is the most appropriate contractual arrangement depends on the particular set of project circumstances. Amongst the most important of these appear to be: the characteristics of the client, the client's requirements and the characteristics of the building project.

CONTRACTS AS A FORM OF ORGANISATION

2.3 One of the basic requirements for the delivery of any construction project is the creation of an effective mechanism for bringing together a wide range of design, construction and other project specialists. Typically, this expertise comes from several different organisations. A key decision for any client is, therefore, what mechanisms he will select to manage these interorganisational relationships. Of the several possibilities which exist, it is believed that contractual arrangements are especially significant.

Table 2.2   Contractual arrangements and client characteristics

Case study number	Client category[1]		Degree of experience[3]		Contractual arrangement
	Primary	Secondary	Experienced	Not experienced	
US1		*	*		Lump sum
US2		*		*	Construction management
US3		*	*		Construction management
US4		*		*	Construction management
US5		*	*		Design-build
US6	*		*		Negotiated guaranteed maximum price (non-competitive)
UK1	*		*		Negotiated (non-competitive)
UK2	*		*		Negotiated (non-competitive)
UK3		*	*		Management contract
UK4		*[2]	*		Negotiated two-stage competitive

Key
[1] A primary constructor is an organisation whose prime aim is to provide construction facilities. A secondary constructor is an organisation whose expenditure on construction is a small percentage of its total turnover.
[2] In UK4, the client is a major design and construction company with worldwide operations, providing construction facilities for others. In this case it is providing offices for itself.
[3] A client is classed as being experienced if he has constructed two or more buildings.

2.4   A contract has been defined as 'a mutual agreement between two or more parties that something shall be done . . . an agreement enforceable by law'[2]. As such, it acts as a device for conducting exchanges with the aim of ensuring predictability and security in business transactions. In commissioning the construction of a facility, a client can select from several types of contractual arrangements which:

a.   appoint the organisations that are to provide him with goods and services;
b.   define their duties and responsibilities and the conditions under which they apply;
c.   specify what is to happen in exceptional circumstances or if there is a failure to perform.

The type of contractual arrangement adopted determines not only the relationship of the various design, construction, and advisory organisations with the client but also their relationships with each other. For example, it establishes the stage at which each is to be involved in the project, the lines of communication and responsibilities for information provision and the pattern of co-ordination and control. Thus, although often regarded as being primarily concerned with defining the role of the building contractor, in practice contractual arrangements have direct and significant implications for all the parties involved in construction project delivery.

2.5   From this perspective, the interest in contracts displayed in this study stems not so much from their status as legal documents, important though this is, but rather from their role in establishing the relationships between the various parties involved in construction projects. Contracts are regarded as representing different organisational arrangements for defining and co-ordinating the contribution of the several bodies involved in construction project delivery[3]. The main differences between these organisational arrangements will be explored in the next section.

COMPARISON OF CONTRACTUAL ARRANGEMENTS
2.6   This section compares the five different forms of contractual arrangement studied. After a brief description of the basic interorganisational arrangements implied by each major contractual type,

the views expressed about their relative merits are summarised. It is not claimed that this comparison is exhaustive nor uncontroversial[4]. Moreover, some of the qualities attributed to particular contracts may appear contradictory. This is because the assessment represents the experience and opinions of those interviewed in the course of the study. The views of these major clients and leading professionals were not always in agreement.

Lump sum contract
2.7   This is generally regarded as being the traditional form of contract on building projects[5]. Here, the client appoints independent consultants to act on his behalf to produce the design and supervise construction. The lump sum contract views project delivery essentially as a sequential process, with design being largely completed before the appointment of the building contractors to whom detailed plans and specifications must be given. Typically, it places the main responsibility for co-ordinating the various organisations with the architect and the building contractor undertakes to perform work for a fixed price. In the UK, this price is adjustable according to a governmentally published set of indices. A fixed period for construction with damages for overrun are often incorporated.

2.8   The three main benefits interviewees associated with lump sum contracts were:

a.   it is simple and familiar and therefore relatively well understood. For this reason, it was an obvious first option considered by many clients;
b.   it establishes a well-defined set of relationships and responsibilities at each stage of the project. Some believe that this leads to greater clarity than several of the other contractual arrangements;
c.   it offers greater price certainty to the client because contractors bid fixed prices on the basis of detailed plans. It, therefore, involves the client in less financial risk.

For all these reasons, it was felt that lump sum contracts can lead to effective project performance, especially if any special requirements for speed and cost are incorporated into building design at an early stage.

2.9   At the same time, however, lump sum contracts were seen as having several major limitations. Among those frequently cited were:

a.   the length of time taken to deliver projects because of the need to complete all design work before letting the construction contracts. Although providing cost security in times of inflation, this extension of time may result in higher bid prices and thus higher overall project costs;
b.   the loss of savings potentially available through earlier involvement of the contractor;
c.   the higher probability of adverse relationships being established between the various parties, especially in projects which undergo a large number of changes. Having agreed a price for building to a defined specification, any variations from this specification are subject to renegotiation between the parties. This process can be time consuming and may delay progress on a project, sometimes creating a conflict of interest between those involved;
d.   the generally lower level of flexibility involved, especially by comparison with the other forms of contract.

Negotiated contracts
2.10   The negotiated contract is perhaps more accurately described as a method of tendering rather than a form of contract. However, because of the way the roles and relationships between the various parties are established, it has been considered as a separate category.

2.11   In negotiated contracts, the client or his representative (in the UK, the quantity surveyor) negotiates a set of conditions and prices with the building contractor on the basis of scheme drawings and specifications. While retaining the traditional role of the architect as co-ordinator of the project team, this form of contract provides for the involvement, and hence contribution, of the contractor early in the project development process.

2.12 Two main benefits were identified:

a. the greater potential for speed associated with the early involvement of the contractor in the design process. In this way, the contractor can:

    i. provide valuable input on the availability of materials and of labour which may influence design decisions;

    ii. consider the sequence of construction so as to avoid or minimise any foreseeable obstacles, such as bad weather seasons;

    iii. plan ahead for long lead items.

b. the possibility for 'fast tracking', ie the overlapping of design and construction. Where this approach is used, negotiated contracts were seen as shortening bid times, thereby enabling an earlier start on site, before completion of design drawings.

Although the greater involvement of the contractor may cost more in fees, it was generally felt that this could be easily offset by the savings. Moreover, as one US client commented, this fee was likely to be less than that incurred through employing a separate construction manager.

2.13 Two disadvantages of negotiated contracts were identified:

a. the greater level of client risk arising from the relative lack of certainty in the final price. This reservation was voiced more strongly in the UK and did not seem to concern the US clients. It led some people to suggest that negotiated contracts might involve the client's consultants in more work in monitoring costs. Alternatively, in one case the client negotiated a Guaranteed Maximum Price and a bonus for early completion. The contractor finished ten weeks ahead of time, was awarded his bonus, and then agreed a price for carrying out the changes the client wanted which fell outside the terms of the original contract;

b. although they were regarded as establishing a context in which adverse relationships were less likely to occur, several interviewees suggested that negotiated contracts could lead to more confusion over roles and responsibilities.

Construction management

2.14 Instead of organising the contribution of different specialists on a sequential basis, construction management treats project planning, design and construction as mutually interdependent tasks. It aims to achieve a higher level of integration by separating managerial from technical (ie designing and building) responsibilities through the appointment of a specialist construction manager. The task of the construction manager, who acts as the client's agent, is to co-ordinate and control all aspects of the project so as to achieve the client's stated requirements. This generally involves considering construction processes simultaneously with design, construction expertise being provided by the construction manager. Construction management is frequently described as a team approach to building since it generally involves the creation of a project group involving the client, construction manager, architect and other consultants and sub-contractors as required. This team is involved throughout the project and led by the construction manager.

2.15 The benefits offered by construction management were described in the following terms:

a. clients have a greater degree of control over the project. Specifically, by having what they regard as a relatively independent construction manager acting as their agent, they are given more information on which to base decisions and are thus able to make more conscious trade-offs between cost, time and quality. This appears especially valuable for the inexperienced client. Although it often places more demands on the client by involving him extensively in project decision making, some clients see construction management reducing the need for the client to take on extra staff for project monitoring and control;

b. it offers a higher probability of achieving project performance within tight time and cost constraints. This in part results from the possibility for phased construction which allows for an early start on site and consequent earlier completion. It also reflects the greater attention given to the interrelationship between design choices and ease of construction and what is generally felt to be the greater degree of flexibility achievable throughout the project;

c. it often establishes a cohesive team rather than a group of adversaries and thus, as a result, it is generally easier to overcome problems without undue delay and bargaining.

2.16 At the same time, several disadvantages were identified:

a. it can make a complicated situation still more complex by adding yet another organisation and another interface to be co-ordinated;

b. it adds a further fee, although some argued that this was offset by a reduction in the management costs of the works contractors;

c. of greater significance was the concern that it involves more uncertainty and hence more risk because it guarantees nothing on price. Moreover, if the professional service is found to be wanting, it was felt that the client has less redress than against a general contractor.

Management contracting

2.17 Under this arrangement, the owner appoints a management contractor, who may be a general contractor, to work alongside the other professional consultants. The aim is to ensure that construction expertise is incorporated into the design at an early stage in the project. The management contractor does not carry out any of the construction but, in addition to advising the design team, is generally responsible for setting up the site establishment, providing general back-up services, advising on the use of specialist sub-contractors and organising construction.

2.18 Because there are many similarities between construction management and management contracting, most of the comments about their benefits were also similar. For example, the client for case UK3, felt that the management contract had facilitated:

a. phased construction, allowing for greater speed of project delivery;

b. maximum competition for each of the (sub)contracts; this resulted in savings which were regarded as more than compensating for the extra fee incurred;

c. the creation of good, harmonious relationships between the various parties.

2.19 However, several important differences were observed between projects organised on the basis of construction management and management contracts[6]. On the evidence of the projects examined, the professional construction manager initiates more and earlier. He tends to be the leader of the design team and provides all the main cost, planning and construction advice. He administers but does not hold the sub-contracts. This is generally the responsibility of the client. By way of contrast, the management contractor in UK3 was not the leader of the team. In terms of cost advice and control he acted in a secondary role to the quantity surveyor. Although he was appointed at a later stage in the project than his counterpart in construction management, he held all the sub-contracts and could thus be regarded as having greater control over them.

Design-build

2.20 In design-build, the client makes an agreement with one single administrative entity, the prime contractor, who is given responsibility for the whole project, from initial briefing through to construction of the building. Unlike the other forms of contract, it involves the contracting organisation becoming the overall co-ordinator and manager of the project team.

2.21   The sample included one project which was managed by design build. The client on this project regarded this form of contractual arrangement as especially suitable for his project because it simplified all important communication and co-ordination channels. He described the benefits in the following terms:

a.   it provided single point responsibility between client and the design-builder;
b.   it eased communications between the various specialist groups who were all part of a single organisation. This clarity and simplicity was felt, by both client and contractor, to have been especially important in this very complex and tightly constrained job;
c.   it was also believed to have provided a high degree of flexibility and response to changes at all stages of the project. This, together with the facility for phasing design and construction, resulted in an early completion time with all its attendant benefits.

2.22   Other interviewees listed similar benefits but at the same time identified three limitations:

a.   they doubted whether this form of contract could ensure high quality of design and construction, since there are fewer in built checks and balances. There might be lack of stimulus for design innovation;
b.   it is more difficult in this form of contract to assess value for money because of the different systems and services offered by different organisations and the limited amount of information available when the contract is awarded;
c.   there is a potential risk of reduced client control and flexibility because there is just one organisation involved in preparing plans, letting sub-contracts etc. It was acknowledged that the potential benefits derived from working with a single organisation can in practice become a major problem should adverse relationships develop between the client and design builder.

Review of comparisons
2.23   Reviewing these comparisons, it is clear that there are several factors which were repeatedly identified as significant considerations in contract selection. These were:

a.   the client's knowledge and experience in commissioning buildings. Construction management and management contracting were often felt to be especially valuable for those with little experience and/or limited in-house building expertise;
b.   requirements for the achievement of tight cost and speed standards. Although possible with lump sum contracts, it was generally felt that the other forms of contract were more likely to achieve tighter standards. This is because they offer the possibility for fast tracking, because they place greater emphasis on the interdependence of design and construction choices, and because they appear more flexible;
c.   risk. Some forms of contract, especially lump sum, were regarded as providing greater price certainty, and hence reduced financial risk. They also appear to offer the client more redress if problems are encountered, although views differed on this;
d.   flexibility. Some contractual arrangements, notably lump sum, were felt to offer significantly less flexibility than others and, hence, to create more obstacles to the implementation of necessary changes. For this reason, the lump sum contract was seen as more prone to conflict and the emergence of adverse relationships between the various parties.
e.   cost. The more parties involved, and the longer their period of involvement, the more costs incurred in fees etc. Thus, lump sum contracts were often regarded as the least costly.

The next section will explore how these factors came together in the sample of ten projects.

FACTORS RELATED TO CONTRACTUAL ARRANGEMENTS

2.24   The purpose of this section is to examine why particular forms of contractual arrangement were selected for those projects studied. Specifically, the cases will be examined to see if they indicate any systematic relationship between contractual arrangements and client characteristics, performmance requirements or project characteristics.

Client characteristics

2.25   The needs of clients are likely to be influenced by two important characteristics:

a.   whether they are primary or secondary constructors. Primary constructors are those clients, such as property developers, whose main business and primary income derive from constructing buildings. Secondary constructors are those for whom expenditure on constructing buildings is a small percentage of their total turnover and for whom buildings are necessary in order to undertake some other business activity, such as manufacturing;

b.   their level of project experience.

The distribution of the sample of clients according to these categories is given in Table 2.2. This table also shows the contractual arrangement which governed their projects.

2.26   On the basis of Table 2.2, it is possible to make the following observations:

a.   lump sum and negotiated contracts were used only by primary constructors or those who could be regarded as experienced clients;

b.   the two inexperienced clients used construction management. In explaining why, both clients emphasised three factors:

  i.   their high performance requirements, in terms of speed of completion. As a result they both perceived a need to work on a fast track basis;

  ii.   their concern to keep flexible relationships in order to keep options open on appropriate design and construction solutions;

  iii.   their desire to maintain a high level of project control by obtaining knowledge, experience or advice which they felt they did not have through their own experience or in-house expertise;

c.   primary clients appeared to prefer negotiated contracts. They saw these as offering scope for fast tracking, ensuring consideration of construction methods in design decisions and the early involvement of the contractor. At the same time, they regarded negotiated contracts as offering greater price certainty than construction management, management contracting or design build. Given their regular commissioning of buildings, primary clients had well established relationships with contractors and thus felt confident that their quality and other requirements would be met.

Performance requirements

Projects vary in the levels of performance to be attained.

2.27   In some cases, there is a requirement for very high performance in respect of speed and/or cost, while on other projects the perceived performance requirement is lower, ie there appears to be more 'slack'[7]. The ten cases were classified according to what those involved regarded as the main project requirements. For those projects described as having low performance demands it should not be assumed that those involved were not aiming for high performance. Rather, in undertaking the project, a tight cost or speed constraint was not identified as a major force driving the project. These project driving forces are summarised in Table 2.3.

2.28   It can be seen that all projects with a clear and tight driving force, either speed or cost, were managed by the non traditional forms of contracting. In all cases, these constraints were identified as a major factor considered in the selection of contractual arrangements.

Table 2.3 Contractual arrangements and performance requirements

	Relative performance requirements	
	Low	*High*
	US1 Lump sum	US2 Construction management – speed
	US6 Negotiated (non-competitive)	US4 Construction management – speed
	UK4 Negotiated (competitive)	US3 Construction management – cost
	UK1 Negotiated (non-competitive)	UK2 Negotiated (non-competitive) – speed
		US5 Design-build – speed
		UK3 Management contract – speed and cost

Table 2.4 Contractual arrangements and project characteristics

		Relative performance requirements	
Relative construction complexity		*Low*	*High*
Low			US2 Construction management
			US4 Construction management
Medium		US1 Lump sum	US3 Construction management
		US6 Negotiated (non-competitive)	UK2 Negotiated (non-competitive)
		UK4 Negotiated (competitive)	
High		UK1 Negotiated (non-competitive)	US5 Design-build
			UK3 Management contract

Project characteristics

2.29 It was considered useful to characterise projects in terms of their relative complexity, believing that this was likely to be at least one important determinant of the need for flexibility. The reasoning here was that more complex projects were likely to be more difficult to manage and to encounter more exceptions. They would thus require a greater need for modifying plans and actions on an ongoing basis.

2.30 In assessing the sample, it was judged that they fell into three recognisable groups, representing different levels of construction complexity and these are described in Table 2.4[8]. Looking at this Table, it is not possible to identify any clear relationship between contractual arrangements and relative construction complexity[9]. What is perhaps of greater interest, is the relationship between complexity and performance requirements.

2.31 Table 2.4 lists the cases according to their performance requirements and construction complexity. It can be seen that there are two projects which can be described as having high performance demands and relatively high complexity. These are US5 and UK3. Both were managed by contractual arrangements which simplifed the co-ordination problems by reducing the number of organisations involved in the project. In US5, this was achieved by appointing a single design-build firm to be responsible for the entire project. In UK3, a great deal of the co-ordination was achieved within the single multidisciplinary design team responsible for the project. In both cases, the contractual arrangements were deliberately selected to ease co-ordination.

Implications

2.32 Because of the relatively small sample of projects, it would be unwise to generalise too far on the basis of these observations. However, the relationships identified in the case studies are consistent with two other sources of data. First, they provide empirical support for many of the opinions expressed by interviewees in their general discussions of contract selection (opinions reviewed in sections 2.6 to 2.23 of this report). Second, moreover, the findings are also consistent with the results of many other studies of organisations, which suggest that complex tasks requiring high levels of performance need to be managed in ways which facilitate the simultaneous consideration of all the interrelated aspects of the problem[10]. Clients would, consequently, be expected to choose those contractual arrangements which they recognised as offering this.

CONCLUSIONS

2.33 Reference has been made to the current debate about the relative merits of different forms of contractual arrangements – a debate which is sometimes articulated in the form of the question: which is the best form of contract for clients? From discussions with major clients and construction professionals and the analysis of the case studies it seems that there may not be a simple answer to this question. Clients differ, their requirements vary and so do the locations in which they build. As a result, they need different buildings and different methods for delivering them.

2.34 The findings of this study suggest that the following are likely to be amongst the most important attributes of projects of relevance to the choice of contractual arrangements:

a. the characteristics of the client, especially his level of experience and his role as a primary or secondary constructor;
b. project requirements, especially any tight cost or speed demands;
c. project characteristics, such as complexity, which make it likely that there will need to be a substantial number of changes in the project, over time.

2.35   Selecting an appropriate form of contract requires careful exploration of each of the above factors and then choice of that contractual arrangement which is particularly suited to the needs and characteristics of the situation. Since each form of contract has both strengths and weaknesses, contract selection involves balancing these against the specific demands of a particular project. It follows, therefore, that there is not one best contractual arrangement but rather which is the most appropriate depends on the particular circumstances of the client and his project[11].

References
1 These contractual types vary according to how responsibilities for design, cost control, planning and construction are defined and allocated.
2 Oxford English Dictionary. These aspects are discussed further in:
    MACAULAY, S. Non-contractual relations in business: a preliminary study. *American Sociological Review.* *28*, pp 55-67;
    EVAN, W.M. Comment on the paper by Macaulay, ibid, pp 67-69;
3 There is now a substantial body of work concerned with the relationship between contract and organisation. Often referred to under the label 'markets and hierarchies', a recent review of this debate is to be found in:
    FRANCIS, A., TURK, J., and WILLMAN, P. (1983). Power, efficiency and institutions. London: Heinemann Educational Books.
4 A detailed description and review of these contractual types are given in Project management in building published by the Chartered Institute of Building, 1982.
5 The term 'traditional' is often used to describe the lump sum form of contract in which the customer has a separate relationship with a design team and a contractor.
    See, for example, The Chartered Institute of Building (1982) Project management in building. Page 7; and NEDO. (1983) Faster building for industry. London: HMSO. Page 3.
6 As there was only one UK case using the management contracting approach, it would be unrealisitic to generalise about these differences.
7 The concept of slack is taken to refer to a situation in which the resources available exceed the minimum required to undertake a particular task. See, for example,
    MARCH, J.G. and SIMON, H.A. (1958). Organisations. New York: J. Wiley;
    CYERT, R.M. and MARCH, J.G. (1963). A behavioural theory of the firm. Englewood Cliffs, New Jersey: Prentice Hall;
8 This assessment of construction complexity took account of such factors as: the characteristics of the site, the number of different trades and the degree of standardisation of construction details and fittings.
9 This may be because we were unable to develop a scale for overall project complexity. The scale of construction complexity used fails to take into account the complexity of the design.
10 See for example:
    THOMPSON, J.D. (1967). Organisations in action. Chicago: McGraw-Hill;
    GALBRAITH, J. (1973). Designing complex organisations. Reading, Massachussets: Addison Wesley;
    VAN DE VAN, A.H., DELBECQ, A.L. and KOENIG, R. (1976). Determinants of co-ordination modes within organizations. *American Sociological Review.* *41*, pp 322-338.
11 This argument parallels that found in more general studies of organisation which have found that the most appropriate form of organisation depends on a number of contextual factors. See for example:
    LAWRENCE, P.R., and LORSCH, J.W. Organization and environment. Boston: Graduate School of Business Administration, Harvard University.
    GALBRAITH, J. (1973), op cit.

3. The management of design and construction

INTRODUCTION

3.1 In the previous chapter it was argued that contractual arrangements are an important mechanism establishing the major organisational relationships between the various parties involved in a particular project. Taking the term 'management' to mean the planning, organising and controlling of projects[1], contracts can thus be regarded as defining the overall project policy within which more detailed project management is carried out.

3.2 Studies of organisations suggest that the mechanisms for project management fall into two very broad categories, as follows[2]:

a. formal systems, such as project planning and control systems, with their associated information and reports. Their main purpose is to specify a blueprint for action which can be easily monitored and appropriate action taken should deviations occur. Once implemented, these blueprints are intended to establish responsibilities in such a way that there is little need for further communication between task performers;

b. personal integrating mechanisms, such as co-ordinating managers and meetings. The purpose of these mechanisms, which are generally regarded as more flexible than formal systems, is to enable mutual adjustment and adaptation through personal discussion and communication[3].

These two categories will be used to describe and analyse the approaches to project management adopted in each of the ten case studies. The main focus will be on the management of these activities across the interfaces between the groups involved in projects rather than within each participating organisation.

PROJECT MANAGEMENT THROUGH FORMAL SYSTEMS

3.3 The main formal systems used for project management derive from planning and programming procedures and their associated reports. The planning process can be viewed as comprising a number of activities as follows:

a. the production of a master plan. This plan identifies the major activities to be carried out. By linking them to a time scale, the plan also specifies the sequence in which they are to be carried out to ensure that design and construction priorities relate to each other to achieve the stated objectives. The master plan provides the overall strategy, defining the bounds within which members of the project team can exercise their own judgement and expertise;

b. the detailed development of the major activities contained in the master plan into a programme, or set of programmes. These provide tactical guidance on what needs to be done, by whom and when;

c. monitoring progress, ie. observing where the project is in relation to the programme and reporting upon it;

d. control. This may follow monitoring and involves taking action upon the information given, particularly if the stated objectives are not being achieved[4]. Such action may lead to subsequent updating, ie. revising the plan and/or programme in the light of the changed circumstances.

One of the aims of the study was to discover how those responsible for projects had planned and controlled either the total project delivery process or their part within it. The following section describes the findings on planning and reporting procedures.

Table 3.1 Planning and programming characteristics – US case studies

Case study no.	US1	US2	US3	US4	US5	US6
PLANNING & PROGRAMMING – contract type	Lump sum	CM	CM	CM	Design build	NC
PRECONSTRUCTION (Design & bid stages) Type of programme	None	CPA	CPA	Linked bar chart	Bar chart	None
No. of Activities	n/a	Unknown	32	25	Unknown	Unknown
CONSTRUCTION Type of programme	CPA	CPA	CPA	CPA	Bar chart	Bar chart
No. of Activities	150	75	132	70	93	30
No. of times monitored	Monthly or weekly	Monthly	Monthly	Monthly	Monthly or fortnightly	Monthly
No. of times updated	None	None	4	None	9	None
If CPA: type used	Activity on arrow	Activity on arrow	Activity on arrow	Precedence	n/a	n/a
Other comments	Bar chart used for trades		Bar charts used from CPA	CPA converted to bar charts		

KEY
n/a = not applicable   CPA = Critical path analysis
CM = Construction management   NC = Negotiated contract

Table 3.2   Planning and programming characteristics – UK case studies

Case study no.	UK1	UK2	UK3	UK4
PLANNING & PROGRAMMING – contract type	NC	NC	MC	NC
PRECONSTRUCTION (Design & bid stages) Type of programme	Milestone dates	Milestone dates	Bar chart	Milestone dates
No. of Activities	n/a	n/a	n/a	n/a
CONSTRUCTION Type of programme	Bar chart	Bar chart	Bar chart	Bar chart
No. of Activities	101	69	91	n/a
No. of times monitored	Monthly	Monthly	Monthly	Monthly
No. of times updated	Unknown	None	None	n/a

KEY
n/a = not available
NC = Negotiated contract
MC = Management contract

Planning procedures
3.4   The approach to planning and planning methods adopted during both preconstruction and construction was considered for each of the cases. The planning characteristics of each project are given in Tables 3.1 and 3.2.

Planning procedures during preconstruction
3.5   The planning techniques used at the design and tender stage ranged in sophistication from none at all to bar charts and network analysis. In the USA, bar charts or CPA were used in four of the six cases. In the UK milestone dates or bar charts were used.
Where bar charts or network analysis were used, the clients had relatively high performance criteria and required an overlap of design and construction activities. In all these cases the contractual arrangement was non-traditional. In the USA, it was either construction management or design build and, in the UK, it was management contracting.

Planning procedures during construction
3.6   The planning procedures adopted during construction were simple bar charts, linked bar charts and network analysis.
In the USA, network analysis was used in four of the six cases. Predictably, the contractual arrangement in three of these four cases was construction management. The bar chart was used in the remaining two cases, for which the contractual arrangements were design-build and negotiated. Monitoring of the programmes was on a one, two or four week period.
In the UK it was possible to obtain detailed information on three of the four cases, all of which used bar charts. In all cases, monitoring took place on a monthly basis.

Use of network analysis
3.7   Network analysis is considered in more detail because its application is of topical interest in the construction industry. The following comments are based on the US case studies (1 to 4) which were the only ones which used network analysis:

a. two types of network analysis were used, precedence diagramming and activity-on-arrow. They were all computer based. One manager also used his own manually prepared network because he thought he achieved a better understanding of the programme;

b. a hierarchy of plans and programmes was developed from the basic network for the differing needs of successive levels of management and trades;

c. the number of activities used in programmes on contracts ranging in value from $2.27m to $42m, varied from 70 to 150.

3.8   The number of activities in a network seemed to be limited for two reasons. Firstly, some managers thought that programmes which were too detailed removed the initiative, expertise and motivation from site supervisory staff and sub-contractors to organize their own work. Secondly, a limited number of activities allowed the manager to understand the relationships between the major activities. Having a network which was easily understood and readily referred to made the manager's daily task of making decisions much easier and more efficient.

3.9   Network analysis was always used by professional construction managers and on those projects which were characterised by relatively high performance requirements.

3.10   Change is often a characteristic of construction work and updating is a procedure for coping with change. However, updating was carried out in only one of the cases. Here, changes affecting the end date led to a revision of the network to accommodate these variations. In this case, network analysis was used for control in the sense of the definition given earlier (paragraph 3.4)[5].

This finding indicates that even where the nature and number of activities had altered over time, there was a marked reluctance to change the networks, even though they were computer based. The reasons given by project managers for this disinclination ranged from the amount of work reprogramming would entail, to the almost certain knowledge that as soon as this revision had been carried out, further changes would invalidate it. Only the most serious variations seemed to warrant an update of the network.

3.11 The low number of activities used in a network combined with the low incidence of updating suggests that network analysis is used primarily to understand the dependencies of activities in the whole project rather than as a scheduling tool.

Reports
3.12 The nature and usage of reports differed both between projects and across the several project phases. For most projects, there were very few formal reports and those were produced on an ad hoc basis. The most common pattern was a construction report, which evaluated progress against the programme on a monthly basis and where appropriate, set out measures for acceleration where delay had occurred.

3.13 There were four cases, all in the USA, which regularly produced more than the normal monthly set of progress meeting minutes.
In one case, the construction manager operated an interesting system of memos which recorded the substance of every conversation and telephone call and provided a detailed file of information and documentation for all those involved in the project. This system was actively used by all members of the team, without additional clerical support.
In another case, during both the design and construction phases, there were weekly reports. These covered a wide variety of topics including progress, costs, weather, potential problems, late drawings etc.

PROJECT MANAGEMENT THROUGH PERSONAL LIAISON
3.14 Planning and programming, together with other formalised control systems, form a crucial part of project management. However, there remain many features of projects which cannot be appropriately controlled through formal systems. They include:

a. those activites which are relatively unstructured or not well understood; this may include the early stages of most projects;
b. those events which are uncertain, unpredictable and unforeseen and which require speedy response;
c. those aspects of projects which require discussion, bargaining and perhaps a measure of compromise[7].

For these it is essential that the relevant people come together to exchange information, opinions and expertise. Thus, personal contacts are a vital element in all project management and allow those involved to adjust to the changing circumstances and requirements of a project as it develops over time.

3.15 People contribute to the management of projects in a number of ways. These range from project liaison or co-ordination by an individual to group meetings[8]. Both individual and collective mechanisms will be considered in the review of the ten projects examined in the course of this study. The detailed findings are to be found in Tables 3.3, 3.4, and 3.5.

Table 3.3   Project co-ordination: design meetings – frequency and organisation attending

Case	Weekly or more often						Less often than weekly						Ad hoc
	Client	Architect	Engineer	Contractor	Construction manager	Other	Client	Architect	Engineer	Contractor	Construction manager	Other	
United States													
US1	*	*	*										*
US2	*	*			*								
US3	*	*			*								
US4							*	*	*		*		*
US5	*	*					*	*	*	*			*
US6						*				*			
United Kingdom													
UK1†							*	*				*	*
UK2							*	*	*	*		*	
UK3	‡	‡	‡				*	*	*	*	*	*	
UK4							*	*	*			*	

KEY
† Internal design meetings were held by multidisciplinary group on weekly basis.
‡ Meetings at all 3 levels of management.

Table 3.4 Project co-ordination: construction meetings – frequency and organisations attending

Case	Weekly or more often						Less often than weekly						Ad hoc
	Client	Architect	Engineer	Contractor	Construction manager	Other	Client	Architect	Engineer	Contractor	Construction manager	Other	
United States													
US1	*	*		*									*
US2	*	*		*		*							
US3†		*			*	*							
US4					*		*	*			*		
US5	*	*				*							
US6	*	*		*		*							
United Kingdom													
UK1							*	*	*	*			
UK2								*	*	*		*	
UK3							*	*	*	*	*		
UK4							*	*	*	*			

KEY
† Meetings at 2 levels of management.

Table 3.5   Overall co-ordination and control – US case studies

Case study no.	A Formal planning			B Meetings			C Client Representative			
	High	Medium	Low	High	Medium	Low	FT	PT	Client employee	External agent
US1D	*			*				*	*	
US1C			*	*			*		*	
US2D	*			*			*		*	
US2C	*			*			*		*	
US3D	*			*			*		*	
US3C	*			*			*		*	
US4D	*				*			*	*	
US4C	*				*			*	*	
US5D		*		*			*		*	
US5C		*		*			*		*	
US6D		*		*			*		*	
US6C			*		*		*		*	

KEY

Column A		Column B			
high	= use of network analysis	high	= weekly or more often	FT	= Full time
medium	= use of bar charts	medium	= weekly to monthly	PT	= Part time
low	= use of milestone dates	low	= less than monthly		

D	=	Design period
C	=	Construction

Table 3.6   Overall co-ordination and control – UK case studies

Case study no.	A Formal planning			B Meetings			C Client Representative			
	High	Medium	Low	High	Medium	Low	FT	PT	Client employee	External agent
UK1D			*		*		*			
UK1C		*			*		*		*	
UK2D			*		*			*		*
UK2C		*			*			*		*
UK3D	*				*			*	*	
UK3C		*			*			*	*	
UK4D			*		*		*	*	*	
UK4C		*			*				*	

KEY

Column A
high   = use of network analysis
medium = use of bar charts
low   = use of milestone dates

Column B
high   = weekly or more often
medium = weekly to monthly
low   = less than monthly

D = Design period
C = Construction

FT = Full time
PT = Part time

Project responsibility within client organisations

3.16 Whilst each of the clients gave specific project responsibility to a particular individual, they differed in the manner in which they did this. In some cases the client's representative had full designated powers and responsibilities while on other projects, he acted primarily as a communication channel, representing the client at meetings but referring back to him on items of significance. A more detailed description of their personal representation is given below.

During design

a. four of the US clients and one UK client appointed full time representatives during the design phase, the others relied on personnel who spent only part of their time acting as project representative.

b. most clients were represented at design meetings by senior in-house personnel. These representatives spent only a proportion of their time on project related activities and generally did not have a construction background. Predictably these were all secondary constructors.

c. two of the primary constructors were represented by in-house personnel who did have a construction background. The remaining primary constructor was represented by an external project manager.

During construction

a. five US and two UK clients appointed full time project representatives.

b. some clients appointed a project manager to act mainly as an expert communication channel, without any formal authority.

c. others used a construction manager, who in addition to acting as a communication channel had delegated authority.

Examination of the data suggests no clear relationship between the method of client representation and other project features.

Group meetings for project co-ordination

3.18 A detailed description of the pattern of meetings for each of the cases is to be found in Tables 3.4 and 3.5[9]. These show that meetings formed part of the regular management of a project. The extent to which they were used varied considerably. Several points emerged from analysis of the case records and from the interviews with project personnel.

a. often there were intensive meetings at the beginning of a project to establish the client's requirements, as in US4. This was especially evident in the US cases where considerable importance seemed to be attached to holding meetings, often lengthy, in order to get a full and detailed understanding of client requirements at the outset of a project;

b. in some cases, the minutes of such meetings replaced formal reports as a control mechanism;

c. overall, the usage of meetings was greatest in US3.[10] This contrasts with the much greater reliance on formal project management systems which characterised US4;

d. during both design and construction, a heavier reliance was placed on meetings in managing the US projects than was the case in the UK projects. In discussing the use of meetings, US interviewees frequently stressed the value of meetings in fostering team spirit and mutual understanding. Other than this, no clear relationship can be observed between use of meetings and other project attributes.

Informal interaction on projects

3.19 From discussions with project personnel it was clear that physical proximity was another significant factor facilitating communication between the various parties. In a number of the projects, representatives of the various organisations were based in the same location, either in the design office or on site. For example, in US5, all the relevant design and build expertise was located within the same building within the same corporation and there was much interaction between the project personnel at all stages. Similarly, in UK3, the multidisciplinary design team achieved a great deal of co-ordination through being next to each other in the same office. In case US3, the client and construction management representatives were both on site, with the architect's office only walking distance away and this was thought to have been of considerable benefit to project progress. This physical proximity enabled informal contact and communication, including during coffee and lunch breaks. This opportunity to 'rub shoulders', was frequently cited as significantly aiding mutual understanding and trust.

OVERALL PROJECT MANAGEMENT
3.20 Tables 3.5 and 3.6 pull together the various elements to give a fuller picture of project management for each of the cases. They relate to the level of sophistication of planning; the level of personal liaison; and client representation[11].

3.21 On the basis of the Tables, the following general observations can be made:

a.   the highest usage of all the co-ordinating mechanisms occurs in US3. The high overall level of project management is a reflection of the effort that was needed in order to achieve the clients unwavering objective to reduce the cost to a level which at first seemed unattainable;
b.   US4 represents a more formalised approach to project management. The management characteristics included an intensive briefing period, followed by substantial monthly reporting, and a memo system. This appeared to be a reflection of both the client's need for formal reports and the style of the particular construction management company involved;
c.   all non traditional contractual arrangements showed a heavy overall investment across the range of project management mechanisms studied. In all such cases, there were relatively high perceived client requirements for speed and/or cost;
d.   it appears that the US projects typically invest more in managing and co-ordinating mechanisms than the UK projects. With one exception, all the high scores on planning, reports, documentation and meetings apply to North American projects.

CONCLUSIONS
3.22 There exists a variety of mechanisms and procedures available for managing projects. These range from formal systems to more personal contacts and include co-ordinating managers and group meetings. How these are used and the emphasis given to each is, in part, a function of the style or preferences of those involved in a project. For example, in one case there was a distinct preference for more formalised procedures while in another there was extensive usage of all co-ordinating mechanisms. However, in addition to personal preferences, two broad patterns were identified:

a.   in five out of the six cases which showed a heavy overall investment in project management, clients had relatively high performance requirements and selected non traditional contractual arrangements. This pattern was true for both US and UK projects. Thus, it would seem that when selecting non-traditional contracts, clients are buying more project management. This is not surprising since an important part of the rationale for such contracts is recognition of the interdependence of the various parties who have to be managed accordingly. Another important part of that rationale is to give additional support to clients where they are either inexperienced or their projects require resources they do not possess or wish to acquire on a long term basis.
b.   there seems to be greater overall investment in project management in the USA than the UK, regardless of contractual arrangements adopted. This is particularly striking in respect of meetings but can also be seen across other procedures for project management.

References

1 This definition represents a common perspective on management, deriving from the work of early theorists on the subject.
For a more extensive discussion of the nature of management, reference may be made to:
GROSS, B.M. (1964). The managing of organizations. New York: Free Press.
MINTZBERG, H. (1973). The nature of managerial work. New York: Harper and Row.
DRUCKER, P. (1977). People and performance. The best of Peter Drucker on management. London: Heinemann.
EARL, M.J. (Ed. 1983). Perspectives on management: a multidisciplinary analysis. Oxford: Oxford University Press.

2 This draws on the basic distinction between formal and personal mechanisms made by MARCH, J.G. and SIMON, H.A. in their seminal work: Organizations. New York: J. Wiley, (1958). It is discussed in more detail in VAN DE VEN, A.H., DELBECQ, A. L. and KOENIG, R. (1976). Determinants of co-ordination modes within organizations. *American Sociological Review 41*, pp 322–338.

3 This aspect is discussed in more detail in THOMPSON, J.D. (1967). Organizations in action. New York: McGraw Hill; and in MINTZBERG, H. (1979). The structuring of organizations. Englewood Cliffs, New Jersey: Prentice Hall.

4 Monitoring and control are often confused. Monitoring is essentially concerned with observing and reporting on past events whereas control involves taking action so as to influence future events.

5 There were a number of criteria for testing usage for control. These included, the number of updates, the ease of access to networks, the comparison between current and previous networks, the familiarity of the site manager with the network and the yellowness of the CPA diagrams on the wall!

6 This is not to say that if there was the opportunity to study projects in the UK using the management contracting arrangement that it would not have found that critical path analysis was more widely used.

7 For a more detailed discussion of this point see:
VAN DE VEN, A.H., DELBECQ, A.L. and KOENIG, R. (1976). op. cit.

8 The various possible ways in which these job responsibilities can be defined are discussed in:
GALBRAITH, J. (1973). Designing complex organizations. Reading, Massachusetts: Addison-Wesley.
MORRIS, P.W.G. (1982). Managing project interfaces: key points for project success. In CLELAND, D.I. and KING, W. R. (Eds) Project management handbook. New York: Van Nostrand Reinhold.

9 These tables include only those meetings which involved people from more than one organisation. Each of the organisations also operated a number of ways of managing and co-ordinating its own activities but these will not be considered because of the primary concern with the integration between the various parties.

10 It is recognised, however, that the analysis under represents the importance of meetings in cases UK3 and US5, in which much of the co-ordination across specialists was done through meetings and discussions within the multidisciplinary team.

11 The three factors are defined as follows:
Column A. The level of sophistication of planning, where;
    high   = use of network analysis
    medium = use of bar charts
    low   = use of milestone dates or no formal procedure.
Column B. The level of personal liaison in terms of frequency;
    high   = weekly or more often
    medium = weekly to monthly
    low   = less than monthly
Column C. The mechanism for representing the client. This has been included because it appears to be an important liaison role; specifically, the amount of attention given to the co-ordination between the organisations is significantly influenced by whether or not the client has a full time representative (with delegated powers) physically located alongside the design and construction personnel.
On the table, the mechanisms have been classified in terms of the following:
    ★ senior management involvement, either full or part time
    ★ client employee acting as project manager, again either full or part time;
    ★ external agent acting as client representative.
Each of these is considered in relation to both the design and construction stages (D and C, respectively).

4. Construction methods

INTRODUCTION

4.1 The approach adopted in this study reflects the assumption that project performance is likely to be a function of the set of human, technical, managerial, organisational and environmental factors involved in any project. Previous chapters have reviewed the organisational and managerial aspects of the project delivery process for the sample of cases examined. This chapter is concerned with the technical details of the construction methods adopted in the projects. It contains a general review of the characteristics of construction methods in the USA and UK and a detailed analysis of the methods used to construct the structural frames of three multi-storey office buildings in the USA and UK.

4.2 It is acknowledged that by concentrating on construction methods and ignoring related design considerations, what follows can only represent a partial view of the technical influences on project delivery. However, the practical limitations of the study reported here precluded the pursuit of a more comprehensive analysis[1].

GENERAL FEATURES OF CONSTRUCTION

4.3 Differences in construction practice for the sample of US and UK projects have been analysed under six main headings; site and structural characteristics, scaffolding, cladding, building services, finishes and fittings. The data for this section are drawn primarily from project documentation and interviews from the main sample of cases. To provide a more general basis it has been supplemented by observations of a number of other buildings in the USA[2] and the authors' experience in the UK. The details of the physical features of the ten projects are listed in Tables 4.1 and 4.2.

Site features

4.4 The most striking difference in the site characteristics of the buildings was the relative amount of space available for construction space beyond the perimeter of the building on the US sites. Even the urban sites were less congested than their counterparts in the UK, thereby allowing the contractor more freedom to construct more easily.

Structural features – a comparison of three buildings

4.5 In order to demonstrate the differences clearly, the structural features of three cases are examined in more detail. The projects which have been chosen share a number of common features, which can be seen in Table 4.3. All three buildings (two in the USA and one in the UK) are office blocks, erected in urban conditions. US6 and UK4 are both reinforced concrete structures, which have approximately the same floor area and were constructed at the same time. These two cases can be directly compared. US3 is discussed because it is an example of steel frame construction.

4.6 a. In US6, the thirteen storey, reinforced concrete frame building comprises a flat waffle slab with circular columns, all of the same size throughout. This allowed the contractor to use prefabricated 'flying forms', which once they were made up on the ground floor, did not need changing nor the addition of any further safety devices. The contractor was also able to pour typical concrete bays of up to 8,200 sq. ft., strike soffits after two days (with repropping), avoid using 'kickers' for the columns, and 'stop ends' and allow the concrete to find its own line after pouring.

b. In UK4, the nine storey reinforced concrete frame building comprises suspended floor slabs with dropped perimeter, spine and lateral beams and columns of differing sizes. This design

Table 4.1   Physical features – US case studies

Study no.	Site features	Structural features	Cladding features	Mechanical service features
US PROJECTS				
US1 OFFICES	Green field rural valley site, 125ft below main road	3 storey RC frame with large span post tensioned slabs acting as inverted pyramid bridge structure, piled foundations	Precast concrete cill units and band of metal framed windows	Air conditioning
US2 FACTORY	Green field site on industrial estate	Single storey, steel frame, pad foundations	Plastic coated metal sheets	Air-conditioning in offices, fans in factory
US3 OFFICES	Green field urban site adjacent to busy highway	16 storey steel frame, piled foundations. Separate multi-storey car park – RC frame	Mirror glass curtain walling. Large tolerance fixing system built into frame	Air-conditioning
US4 WAREHOUSE	Green field rural site	Single storey steel frame on pad foundations	RC tilt up panels cast on site	Cold store system where necessary. Air conditioning in offices.
US5 FACTORY	Urban location. Existing facilities to be extended whilst maintaining current manufacturing operations	Single storey steel frame on pad foundations	Plastic coated metal sheets	Natural ventilation. Fans in factory
US6 OFFICES	Chemical factory & its toxic wastes had to be removed from this urban site	14 storey RC frame, flat slab on precast concrete piled foundations	Brickwork glazed metal frame windows	Air conditioning

Table 4.2   Physical features – UK case studies

Study no.	Site features	Structural features	Cladding features	Mechanical service features
UK PROJECTS				
UK1 SHOPS & OFFICES	Very restricted urban site with many services surrounding it; also planning & operating restrictions	6 storey RC frame on piled foundations suspended slab with dropped edge beam	Brickwork around office area. Opaque panels & glazed metal frame windows around shops	Air-conditioning in shopping area
UK2 OFFICES	Green field site in semi-rural situation	4 storey RC frame on pad foundations, slab with dropped beam around edge. (2 No Blocks)	Brickwork, glazed metal framed windows	Natural ventilation. Hot water radiators
UK3 OFFICES	Green field site adjoining another similar building	7 storey RC frame on piled foundations precast concrete flooring units	High quality opaque panels and glazed metal frame windows	Natural ventilation. Hot water radiators
UK4 OFFICES	Congested urban site with similar adjacent building	9 storey RC frame on pad foundations, suspended slab with dropped edge beam	Opaque panels, double glazed metal frame windows	Air-conditioning

Table 4.3 Methods of construction: characteristics of structural frame of three projects

1	COUNTRY	UK	US	US
2	Case study number	UK4	US6	US3
3	Type of structural frame	Reinforced concrete	Reinforced concrete	Steel
4	Total area of suspended floor	220,000 sq ft	230,000 sq ft	385,000 sq ft
5	Number and area of floors	9 @ 23,400 sq ft each approx	4 @ 20,500 sq ft each 9 @ 16,400 sq ft each	16 @ 24,000 sq ft each approx
6	Construction period for structural frame	March-December 1980 40 weeks	April-November 1980 31 weeks	February-October 1980 36 weeks
	CONSTRUCTION CYCLE			
7	Average number of working days/floor	22 days	14 days and 11 days	11 days
8	Average number of sq ft produced/week	5,500	7,400	10,700
9	Area of typical concrete pour in sq ft	1,722	8,200	12,000
10	Minimum striking time for soffits (with repropping)	7 days	2 days	n/a
11	Type of formwork	Span form, lattice beam adjustable props	Prefabricated metal flying forms	Metal trough permanent formwork
	CONCRETE			
12	Strength @ 28 days	4000 psi	4000 psi	n/a
13	Use of additives	Plasticizer	Air entrainment	n/a
14	Working slump	4 inches	4 inches	n/a
	OTHER			
15	Floor finish	Tamped then screed	Power floated	Power floated
16	Construction of fire escape staircase	In-situ reinforced concrete	Prefabricated steel staircase	Prefabricated steel staircase

limited the contractor to the use of traditional formwork, in this case, of span forms, lattice beams and adjustable props which needed to be erected and dismantled for each pour on each floor. The contractor was also constrained by a maximum pour area of 1,722 sq ft (approximately one fifth of the area permitted in US6) a minimum striking time of 7 days, 'kickers' having to be used for the columns, and 'stop ends' being mandatory.

   c.   In US3, the project is a 16 storey steel framed building. The simple design achieved by incorporating metal trough permanent formwork, eliminated the use of any temporary formwork and much of the steel reinforcement[3].

4.7 The clearest difference between US6 and UK4 lies in the relative simplicity of the method of construction of the structural frame in the USA. In US6 the design of the structure was simplified and standardised for simple and rapid construction. The reinforced concrete frame was designed so that the floor module and dimensions of the structural members did not vary from floor to floor. The flat slab configuration allowed the use of 'flying forms', which also eliminated the use of external scaffolding. Additionally, the facility to pour larger bays of concrete, reduce the striking time of the formwork and eliminate the use of 'kickers' or 'stop ends' further enhanced the speed and economy of construction. These measures are a general characteristic of structural frames in the USA.

4.8 In UK4, the structural engineers had little choice in the form of the structural frame, since they were constrained by the storey height of the adjacent building and the need for ventilation ducts above the false ceiling.

Structural features – general observations

4.9 In UK3 the design team set out to achieve economy of construction by repetition and prefabrication. Accordingly, the grid was standardised and all the horizontal structure was precast concrete ensuring speed of erection (there were only two types of precast concrete units), dry construction and high quality finish. Thus, where construction requirements have been taken into account in the design of buildings in the UK, the results have been good.

4.10 Apart from UK3 the other UK buildings adopted structural systems which were relatively complicated. For UK1 and UK4, the structural engineers had little choice, since they were constrained by planning constraints, foundation conditions and the storey heights of adjacent buildings. In UK2 it was difficult to see why the complicated structural system was adopted.

4.11 A preliminary review indicates that planning restrictions and the foundation material (clay in the UK and rock in the US) limits the height of buildings in the UK, so that more economical and speedy structural frame construction is often excluded.

4.12 In the USA simplicity seemed to be the overriding rule in the form and detail of the structure, whether it was steel or reinforced concrete. In multi-storey buildings, the form was repeated exactly on every floor and the detailing allowed for ease and large constructional tolerances. The large bay prefabricated 'flying forms' were used not only on both the concrete framed US office buildings but this practice was commonly adopted on many other buildings and accounted for the remarkable construction times of between 3 and 14 days achieved for each floor cycle.

Scaffolding

4.13 Another major and readily apparent difference between the USA and UK is the relative lack of external scaffolding used in the USA during the erection of the frame or cladding. Whilst this is comparable with the UK on taller buildings, even the relatively low-rise US buildings did not use scaffolding during the construction of the frame, because flying-forms were used.

Cladding features

4.14 Simplicity was again the predominant theme of the cladding systems in the USA. Where curtain walling systems were used, there was a limited number of types, the tolerances were large and they could be erected without the use of external scaffolding. UK3 compared favourably in that there were a limited number of panel types, but the tolerances were smaller and external scaffolding was used. The fixing details in the USA visibly showed large tolerances, of the order of two inches between cladding panels and the external face of the edge beam.

4.15 In the USA, the only brick bond seen was stretcher bond. The usual problem at windows was avoided by separating the band of windows from the band of brickwork, thereby eliminating the need for tight tolerances and a high degree of skill which was reportedly in very short supply in the masonry trades in the USA.

Building services features

4.16 There was no fundamental difference in the types of building services systems in the two countries. There was however a great difference in the trade practices. In the USA, once the sprinkler system had been installed it was followed by the trunking for the air-conditioning, which was usually prefabricated with flexible connections designed to be plugged into the grilles and installed by the ceiling fixer. Similarly, the electrical services were designed to be erected as far as possible by the electrician, leaving a flexible connection for the ceiling fixer to make to the light fitting. Return visits by those trades were eliminated. All the tradesmen involved worked on mini-stilts. No scaffolding was used for any internal trades associated with normal storey height ceilings. This was common practice on every site visited in the USA. Apart from prefabrication of air-conditioning trunking, none of the UK cases used any of the practices just described. In contrast in UK2 and UK4 special fittings had to be manufactured to comply with the tight floor to ceiling heights.

4.17 The other major difference was in the size and position of the services ducts in the structure. In the USA, these services holes always seemed large in comparison with those in the UK, with the result that the services were erected quickly and simply, without having to use the traditional 'shoehorn' approach common on many UK buildings.

Finishes and fittings

4.18 There are further differences in the operations which follow the completion of the structure. In all US cases there were no 'wet trades', all the partitions being 'sheet rock' or plasterboard. This is a very quick operation, whereby metal studding is fixed to the floor with power tools and the plasterboard is fixed to one side. Sub-contractors often use laser devices to position the walls. Any services are then installed and the sheet rock erector returns to insert the fibreglass and the board on the other side. Jointing is started the next day and final decoration can begin three or four weeks later.

4.19 There were two other operations in the USA which were different. All fire escapes were prefabricated steel staircases, whereas in the UK they were normally cast in-situ concrete and hence slower to construct and potentially more hazardous during construction. In all US cases, the concrete slab was power floated to a smooth finish ready for whatever floor finishes were specified. In contrast three of the four UK cases used screeded floors and plastered walls.

4.20 In the US projects, all fittings were taken from standard ranges readily available, with manufacturer's names, addresses and stock numbers included in the specification. (They were not, however, nominated suppliers). The fittings ranged from door sets, window sets, to sanitary ware and fire escape staircases etc. An example of the standardisation can be demonstrated by the fact that only two types of door frame were observed in all the buildings visited.

4.21   Where false ceilings were used in the USA, they were all chosen from standard catalogues. The ceiling contractor fixed his supporting grid after the services sub-contractor's sprinkler system and primary trunking. The ceiling tiles on all US cases were of the 'lay-in' variety which allowed the contractor the flexibility of leaving the fixing of the ceiling tiles to the end, thereby avoiding damage and maintaining the quality of the tiles.

4.22   In contrast, in UK4 (in common with the many other similar buildings in UK) there were special fittings made to comply with design requirements. Additonally, there were return visits for all the trades mentioned above and scaffolding for the ceiling trades.

CONCLUSIONS
4.24   The case study data and the evidence obtained from viewing a number of buildings in the USA on a less rigorous basis, when combined with the authors' general experience of construction in the UK, suggest the following conclusions on construction methods:

a.   the overall design of buildings in the USA takes account of construction requirements to achieve ease, speed and economy of construction. This is typified by all the US projects which have simple structural frames, simplified finishing processes and standardised components, including greater use of 'off the shelf' components[4];

b.   in the UK, design does not generally appear to be as clearly oriented towards construction requirements, with a consequent loss of performance in ease and speed of construction. However, where there is a conscious attempt to simplify construction processes through building design, as in UK3 which was characterised by a great deal of prefabrication, standardisation of components and elimination of wet trades, construction can be made significantly easier.

References
1 Information on design and construction procedures can be found in other US/UK comparisons. See, for example:
   DEPARTMENT OF CONSTRUCTION MANAGEMENT, UNIVERSITY OF READING (1979). UK and US construction industries: a comparison of design and contract procedures. London: Royal Institute of Chartered Surveyors.
   NEDO. (1983). Faster building for industry. London: HMSO.
2 During the course of the field work in the USA, a large number of buildings and construction sites were photographed. These included not only the projects in the sample of cases but also a much wider range of buildings at various stages of completion. In each of the states and cities visited, wherever possible, the opportunity was taken to talk to site staff in order to obtain a more general impression of construction practice.
3 It is acknowledged that with recent changes in London concerning fire protection of steel framed buildings (as at Cutlers Court), steel will be used more often.
4 It is recognised that the size of the construction market in the USA provides a larger and more stable demand than in the UK. It has been estimated that the US construction industry is approximately fourteen times greater in respect of new work than the UK construction industry. This factor clearly has some bearing on the range and quantity of standardised components. But this alone does not not explain the differences.

5. The vexed question of project performance

INTRODUCTION

5.1   This report began by observing that there is a great deal of interest in the performance of the construction industry. In the work reported here, the intention has been to explore three features of projects: contractual arrangements, the management of design and construction and construction methods. The aim throughout has been to understand how and why particular choices are made in respect of each feature by examining a small sample of recently completed projects and by talking to a number of leading people actively involved in the industry.

5.2   While recognising the limitations of the sample, this chapter will review the cases to see what light they throw on the matter of project performance. The case data will be supplemented by the comments made by those interviewed when discussing the influences on project performance.

WHAT IS PROJECT PERFORMANCE?

5.3   Project performance is an assessment or evaluation of project delivery. It is generally seen as some combination of three factors: speed, ie the time taken from inception to completion; cost, ie the final price paid for a building; and quality, ie the standard of design and construction attained[1]. Discussions in the course of this study identified two factors to be taken into account in any consideration of performance.

Project success is a subjective as well as objective assessment

5.4   Whether or not a project is regarded as successful depends on whether it achieves what is required or expected. Success is, therefore, in large part a function of the needs and expectations of the relevant parties. Thus, although in absolute terms one job may take longer to complete than another similar job, this does not necessarily imply that those involved on the former will be less satisfied than those on the latter. Discussions did not reveal any clear relationship between reported satisfaction and performance assessed in absolute terms (eg cost per square foot; area per week during construction as in Table 5.1). What was more important was that the requirements and expectations of the client were met[2].

Project experiences may influence project assessment

5.5   Evaluations of speed, cost and quality focus primarily, if not exclusively, on the finished project, ie on the eventual outcome. An additonal factor, which may be closely related to outcomes but which was regularly identified separately was the time and energy consumed in the process of project delivery. What might be called the 'hassle factor' may be less visible when the project is finished but may be an important component of the overall assessment of a project by those most closely associated with it.

5.6   For these reasons, it is believed that the question of what is a successful project may be more complex than it appears and that the answers may be more difficult to establish than is often suggested.

LEVELS OF PERFORMANCE

5.7   From the individual case descriptions provided in the Appendix, it is apparent that most of the projects were assessed by those involved as being relatively successful. At the same time, however, it is clear that there were variations in the speed, cost and quality.

5.8 Because of the difficulty of establishing comparable criteria for assessing the quality of design and construction, comment is restricted to speed and cost performance. Tables 5.1 and 5.2 present each case on the two dimensions of speed and cost. These Tables, together with the interview data, provide the basis for the following discussion of project performance.

Speed of construction

5.9 From Tables 5.1 and 5.2, it is clear that, in common with the findings of other studies, the US buildings were constructed faster than those in the UK. With one exception, all the US jobs had a construction speed in excess of 2500 feet per week, whereas all the UK jobs fell well below this figure.

5.10 There are several reasons for this difference. For example, the US jobs were all larger, bringing with them economies of scale, including prefabrication and higher levels of standardisation[3]. Second, the cases are not all strictly comparable, some of them being manufacturing and warehousing facilities

Table 5.1   Project performance – details

Case Study No	Function	Area (sq ft) gross	Construction time (weeks)	Final construction cost	Cost/sq ft†	Area/week during construction (sq ft)
US INDUSTRIAL						
US2	Manufacturing facility	53,000	30	$2.3m	$43 (£24)	1766
US4	Warehouse	360,000	100	$34.8m	$97 (£54)	3600
US COMMERCIAL						
US1	Corporate offices	440,000	130	$42m	$95 (£53)	3385
US3	Corporate offices	385,000	143	$24m	$62 (£34)	2692
US6	Speculative offices	230,000	69	$14.4m	$56 (£31)	3333
UK COMMERCIAL						
UK1	Speculative shops & offices	130,000	134	£8.7m	£67	970
UK2	Speculative offices	72,000	78	£2.9m	£40	923
UK3	Speculative offices	127,000	78	£8.2m	£64	1628‡
UK4	Corporate offices	220,000	108	£10.9m	£50	2037

† The then currency exchange rate of $1.8=£1.00 has been used.
‡ includes building 400 car parking garage beneath offices.
Note: US5 is not included in this table because comparable performance figures were not available.

Table 5.2 Project performance – cost and speed

| | | Speed | | |
		High	Medium	Low
	Low	US6	US2 US3	UK2
Cost	Medium	US1 US4	UK4	
	High	UK3	UK1	

KEY
Speed   High = < 3000 sq ft per week during construction
           Medium = 1500-3000 sq ft per week during construction
           Low = < 1500 sq ft during construction

Cost   Low = < £45 per sq foot
           Medium = £45-60 per sq foot
           High = >£60 per sq foot

       Note: US5 has been omitted from this table because no comparable performance figures were available.

while others are office developments. It should also be pointed out that in the United States, speculative developers only construct the shell, essential services, toilets and lobbies, whereas UK developers provide a finished office area, including floor, wall and ceiling finishes ready for a tenant to move in. However, for the three most similar buildings, US3, US6 and UK4, the US projects were completed faster and at lower cost.

5.11 Further analysis of the data suggests that there are few other features which can be clearly and systematically related to speed as measured here. Thus, for example, the cases show that fast results can be achieved with all forms of contract and that good performance can be achieved even when there is not a strong perceived requirement, or driving force, for fast completion. What is clear, however, is that those jobs which were constructed quickly, were ones in which the client made a substantial investment in project management. This was achieved either through strong client involvement and representation (US1 and US6) or through the use of construction managers (US3 and US4).

5.12. When those involved in the 'faster' projects were asked about their projects, they identified four factors as being especially important influences:

a. the knowledge and experience of the client together with his ability to make decisions quickly;
b. the contractual arrangements; these either gave the architect time to prepare a detailed brief or established flexible arrangements permitting quick responses to changes;
c. the good working relationships between the main parties to the contract;
d. the simplification and standardisation of construction features.

5.13 In the course of the study, a number of general questions were asked about what people thought were the crucial factors affecting the speed of project delivery. The responses were as follows:

a. the US respondents clearly thought that the availability of materials, sub-contractors and labour, plus the weather, to be the most crucial factors. By contrast, these were not mentioned by the

UK respondents, who thought that the design and construction process was the most important. This is paradoxical given the evidence of the case studies which shows that there was a great deal of attention given to the relationship between design and construction and overall project management on all US projects. It may be that these aspects are more taken for granted in the USA and that the US respondent placed greater emphasis on what they regarded as 'less controllable' project elements. It may also be that the current debate about design and construction in the UK has heightened awareness of its importance;

b.   all interviewed thought that the characteristics of the client, his clarity of objectives and ability to make decisions, were of considerable importance.

Cost of construction

5.14   The spread of cost performance across the cases is relatively wide, ranging from £24 per square foot to £67 per square foot. Once again, a large proportion of this variance can be explained by major differences in the nature of the buildings.

5.15   The differences between the performance of US and UK projects is not so marked on cost as it is on speed, although for the three most similar cases, US3, US6 and UK4, the costs of construction are less in the USA than the UK. As with speed of construction, effective cost performance seems to be achievable with all forms of contractual arrangement. Also, speed does not necessarily have to be achieved at the expense of cost. The fastest jobs did not cost the most.

5.16   Two factors in particular were identified as contributing to good performance on the low cost projects. These were:

a.   contractual arrangements. For construction management contracts, these were seen to provide the client with regular and detailed information on the cost implications of decisions, sometimes through value engineering, and to provide the flexibility to implement changes without delay or difficulty. Negotiated contracts also allowed flexibility and early consideration of construction in the design process and, like management contracts, were seen as conducive to good working relationships between the parties to the project;

b.   simplicity and standardisation of design.

5.17   As with speed of construction, interviewees were asked more general questions about the influences on the costs of building. In these discussions, several differences between the USA and UK emerged:

a.   it was clear that there was a much greater emphasis on the use of standard products and fittings in the USA. Given the substantial size of the US building market, this standardisation was thought to reduce costs. It may also account for the greater emphasis placed by the US interviewees on the importance of materials availability in relation to speed;

b.   US respondents implied that there was a much stricter discipline in respect of change and variation orders. Where these do occur, the cost and time implications are discussed and agreed with the client before they are implemented. It was thus felt that by making the cost implications of change more visible, variations were kept to a minimum. Although UK respondents agreed on the importance of this factor, they did not appear to enforce the same degree of control over the introduction of changes.

CONCLUSIONS

a.   Office buildings are designed and constructed more quickly in the USA than in the UK. At the same time, there appears to be a smaller difference in the costs of office buildings[4].

b. Fast building is possible without sacrificing cost[5].
c. The following are important influences on performance:

    i. the vital role of the client in providing substantial and appropriate management input[6];
    ii. selection of the appropriate contractual arrangements[7];
    iii. simplicity and standardisation of design and construction methods[8].
    iv. the late introduction of changes into a project[9];

Although based on a small sample of projects, the findings reported here are consistent with those of recent comparative studies of US and UK construction practice.

References
1 This is the view generally taken in the following reports:
NEDO. (1976). Engineering construction performance. London. HMSO.
DEPARTMENT OF CONSTRUCTION MANAGEMENT, UNIVERSITY OF READING. (1979).
UK and US construction industries: a comparison of design and contract procedures. London: Royal Institution of Chartered Surveyors.
2 It is possible that when assessing individual projects clients appear to attach greater importance to project effectiveness, ie the achievement of their stated objectives, than to efficiency, ie the level of resources used to those objectives.
3 The difficulties involved in making comparisons of this sort are reviewed in FREEMAN, I.L. (1981). Comparative studies of the construction industry in Great Britain and North America: a review. Watford: Building Research Establishment.
4 The University of Reading Report, (1979 op. cit.) for example, found that office buildings were designed and constructed much more quickly in the USA than the UK but discovered no significant difference in the total construction costs of office buildings in the USA and UK. The Slough Estates Reports (1976 and 1979) op. cit.) also found that time performance in the UK was markedly inferior to that in the USA and, indeed, a number of other countries too.
5 See, for example, NEDO. (1983) Faster building for industry. London: HMSO
6 This factor receives considerable emphasis in;
FREEMAN, I.L. (1981). op. cit; NEDO (1983) op. cit. and in The manual of the British Property Federation system for building design and construction (1983). London: British Property Federation.
7 The recent NEDO Report found as follows: 'While traditional methods of design and tendering can give good results, on average non-traditional techniques tend to be quicker, and within the traditional approach, both tendering on bills of approximate quantities and choice of contractor with a negotiated tender lead to faster progress.' Faster building for industry. op. cit. p.4.
8 This has been suggested by several reports including: The Reading Report (1979) op. cit.; the NEDO Report (1983) op. cit.
9 An observation also made in the Reading Report (1979). op. cit.

6. Reflections and future directions

INTRODUCTION
6.1 The opening chapter of this report explained that the aim was to undertake a study which would allow examination and comparison of the organisational, managerial and technical factors involved in a sample of US and UK building projects. The subsequent chapters have reviewed the findings on each of these topics and then considered them in relation to overall project performance.

6.2 The study throws light on several matters which are of current concern in the building industry. In this context, the findings can be encapsulated in two points:

- many of the observations support other recent comparative studies which suggest that the US construction industry performs better in some respects than the UK industry. In exploring this further, it has been found that there is not one but several factors which may account for this difference. Within the scope of this project, these are seen as including general environmental factors, such as planning regulations, site characteristics and construction methods as well as the general approach to project management adopted. It is particularly in respect of the organisation and management of projects that this study suggests new avenues for further exploration.
- regardless of country location, the project delivery process is best understood as a set of highly interdependent activities. For example, it has been shown that the selection of contractual arrangements appears to be a function of the type of client, his time and cost requirements and the characteristics of his project. Those projects which demonstrated a high level of project management were characterised by relatively high performance requirements and the use of non traditional contractual arrangements. This interdependence of factors is represented in Figure 6.1[1]. It is only a partial representation of project delivery, since it leaves out a number of other important influences, not least the characteristics of the people involved in projects. It does, however, summarise the main relationships between the factors examined in the course of the study.

6.3 The study has direct and important implications for all those with an interest in building projects. These will now be reviewed in relation to clients, those in the industry and those considering possible directions for future research.

IMPLICATIONS FOR CLIENTS
6.4 The study emphasises the significance of three activities for all clients:

- the development of clear and widely understood objectives. Performance requirements specified by clients have important implications for both the selection of contractual arrangements and the approach to project planning adopted. Thus, it is vital that clients achieve a clear understanding of their project goals as early as possible. Almost every interviewee attributed the greatest significance to the influence of this factor on project delivery;
- examination of in-house experience and ability in managing projects. Where clients do not have the experience or appropriate level of in-house expertise to manage a project, they should select one of the non-traditional forms of contractual arrangement in order to have the advice of a person experienced in the industry acting as their agent;
- a continuing commitment to project management. Whatever forms of contractual arrangement and project management approaches are selected, there appears to be no substitute for the

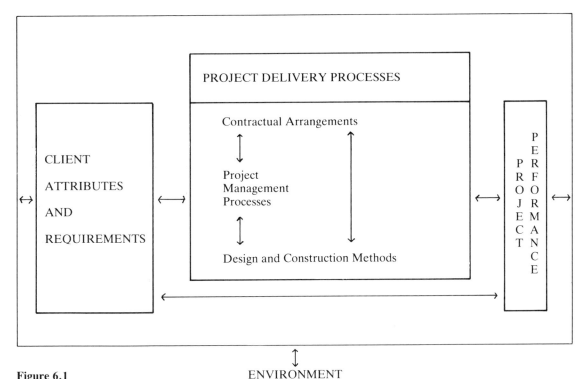

Figure 6.1   ENVIRONMENT

investment of time and energy by clients. The one feature which stands out in the successful projects is the considerable commitment by clients to involvement in their projects. This does not mean involvement in the minutae of projects, but the ability to make decisions quickly when unforeseen problems arise.

IMPLICATIONS FOR THE INDUSTRY
6.5
- The search for the one best way to manage all projects is likely to be fruitless. Rather there is a need for several different approaches to suit the characteristics of different clients and different projects. It follows that an important skill for those working in the industry is the ability to match the various approaches to the particular attributes and requirements of clients and their projects.
- The implications of this 'best-fit' approach is that the trend towards diversification of project management approaches, both within and between organisations, is likely to continue. As a result, many individuals and organisations are likely to find themselves working in new patterns of relationship with other parties in the industry.
- There may be much to be learned by looking at design, construction and management practice in other countries. Clearly, not all is transferable but many aspects, such as the greater application of standardisation, may be.

IMPLICATIONS FOR RESEARCHERS
6.6 Considerable importance is attached to the continued study of building projects as a basis for increasing the knowledge of the factors influencing effective performance. Although not a compre-

hensive list, the study suggests that there is likely to be particular value in further exploration of the following four factors[2]:

- Clients and client organisations:
  In the light of the growing awareness of the significance of the client in influencing project delivery, it is crucially important to extend the knowledge and understanding of the different needs of clients. This is likely to include:

  i. greater appreciation of the processes whereby clients develop their building requirements and objectives;
  ii. identification of what types of project support and advice are appropriate for different types of client across the various stages of their projects.

- Interface management, including:

  i. contractual arrangements. Since these can be regarded as establishing the strategic framework within which project delivery takes place, further appreciation of the benefits and costs they offer to clients and other parties can only be of value;
  ii. personal integrating mechanisms, including liaison roles and meetings. The US projects used meetings to a far greater extent than UK projects and this was especially true in the early stages of a project. Project startup is increasingly recognised as a particularly critical stage in project management which is, as yet, relatively little researched[3].

- The role of formal planning systems in project management:
  Observations have been made on the use of different approaches to planning and programming. Given the current developments in information technology, this is potentially a significant area of change.
- Building design and construction methods:
  The aim here would be to explore the potential benefits and costs of further standardisation and simplification.

6.7 To be effective, such studies will require extensive collaboration between all those involved in commissioning and delivering buildings. However, it is only through careful analysis of ongoing projects, from their very earliest stages through to completion, that it will be possible to develop a well-founded understanding of the real influences on project delivery.

References
1 It will be apparent that this figure resembles the models to be found in analyses of projects within a systems perspective. See, for example,
   NAHAPIET, H.N. and NAHAPIET, J.E. (1982). Project characteristics, contractual arrangements and the organisation of construction. Working Paper of the Oxford Centre for Management Studies;
   CLELAND, D.I. and KING, W.R. (1983, 3rd edition). Systems analysis and project management. McGraw Hill.
   MORRIS, P.W.G. (1983). Managing project interfaces – key points for project success, in Cleland, D.I. and King, W.R. (eds) Project management handbook. Van Nostrand Reinhold.
2 It is recognised that some of these investigations are already underway, many of them supported by grants from the Science and Engineering Research Council's Specially Promoted Programme In Construction Management.
3 The International Project Management Association currently has a working group on Project Startups. The topic is also referred to in MORRIS, P.W.G. (1983) op cit.

Case descriptions

INTRODUCTION

This appendix provides a short case history for each of the ten projects examined in the course of the study. The material is presented in a standard format under the following main headings.

CASE DESCRIPTION: Each case is identified by its country and sample project number. This is followed by brief case details describing:

a.   the type of building, ie. offices or industrial premises;
b.   the location;
c.   the value in millions (pounds or dollars depending on location) at time of completion;
d.   the construction period in months.

TYPE OF CLIENT: Clients have been described in terms of three categories:

a.   Public or private sector;
b.   Primary or secondary constructors. Primary constructors are those whose main business and primary income derive from building construction, whereas secondary constructors are those for whom buildings are necessary in order to undertake some other business activity;
c.   Experienced or inexperienced. For the purposes of this study a client who had carried out at least two construction projects within the previous five years was defined as 'experienced'.

CLIENT REQUIREMENTS: This identifies the main project performance requirements in terms of cost, speed or quality.

CONTRACTUAL ARRANGEMENT: Describes the contract type used to manage the project.

CLIENT TEAM: Describes both the client's internal arrangements for managing the project and the mechanisms linking the client with the other parties involved.

PROJECT PLANNING AND CONTROL: Describes the approach to project planning and control adopted during preconstruction and construction.

DESIGN AND CONSTRUCTION SOLUTION: Describes the primary physical characteristics of the building.

ASSESSMENT: Provides a general evaluation of the project based on the assessments of those involved.

CASE DESCRIPTION   US1

OFFICES   ALABAMA $42m   30 months

1   TYPE OF CLIENT: Public utility company, primary constructor, experienced.

2   CLIENT REQUIREMENTS: The company, being sensitive to public opinion, required its Alabama based corporate headquarters to demonstrate clear commitment to energy conservation and to cause minimal environmental impact on a green field rural site. Quality of design was the main requirement. Although there was a deadline to meet when the lease expired on its existing offices, speed was not regarded as a major problem. Cost was the least important performance criterion.

3   CONTRACTUAL ARRANGEMENT: Lump sum competitive bids, limited to locally based companies.

4   CLIENT TEAM: The client used an in-house project manager who had considerable experience of the construction industry. Internally, the client's representative held numerous meetings with many departments in the company to determine their requirements. This seemed to be the most problematic part of his job but, in the event, it generated few variations. His executive powers and seniority allowed him to make decisions very quickly.
    The client had a contract with the architect who in turn had contracts with the various consulting engineers. The contractor was appointed through an orthodox competitive tendering process.

5   PROJECT PLANNING AND CONTROL: At the preconstruction stage no formal planning was used. At the construction stage a critical path analysis was used. It was monitored and updated monthly. Bar charts were compiled for each trade.
    There were few reports, but meetings were held at least fortnightly throughout the project, with the client's representative taking an active role with consultants and contractor.

6   DESIGN AND CONSTRUCTION SOLUTION: The project design was selected in through a design competition. It produced a solution involving a bridge-like inverted pyramid structure spanning a valley. The design incorporated a number of passive energy conservation features and, through a scheme of tree planting on the roof, blended well into the surrounding countryside and woods. The structure was a standard bay, large span reinforced concrete frame.

7   ASSESSMENT: The client, consultants and contractor were all pleased with the project. The client moved on time into a building which achieved his design objectives and which was approved by the community. The following factors were identified as contributing to this success.

    a.   the client had a representative who was knowledgeable, experienced and had the power to make decisions quickly;
    b.   the architect, with an early precise brief, had enough time to prepare the design adequately and the opportunity to meet the client's representative regularly to obtain approvals;
    c.   the contractor's supervisor, who was very experienced, had worked with the architect and client on a previous project and had good relationships with them. The supervisor was pleased because the repetitive nature of the structure and finishes gave him the opportunity to standardise his production cycle and hence operate profitably.

CASE DESCRIPTION US2

FACTORY GEORGIA $2.3m 7 months

1 TYPE OF CLIENT: Subsidiary of a major Japanese manufacturer of electronic equipment, secondary constructor, inexperienced in USA.

2 CLIENT REQUIREMENTS: The client wanted to set up a manufacturing facility in the USA, which would be operational by a particular date. This was 13 months from the date of appointment of the consulting architect/engineer practice. Whilst speed was the most important criterion, the quality of the workplace for the operatives was also important.

3 CONTRACTUAL ARRANGEMENT: Although originally set up on a lump sum contract, the consultants recommended adoption of a construction management arrangement in order to achieve the tight design and construction deadline. This contract enabled the project to be constructed on a fast track basis.

4 CLIENT TEAM: The client was represented by the designated manager of the proposed facilities. He coordinated decision making in the many internal committees and communicated with the design team. In the early stages of the design, this manager was based in Tokyo. His remoteness, together with the language difference, led to a number of early problems and misunderstandings. However, these were overcome when he moved to Georgia permanently.
The client appointed a firm of Japanese/American consultants to prepare the brief for the American consultants. This local multi-disciplinary design team had all the major disciplines within their own organisation. The contractors were appointed on a lump sum contract, awarded after competitive tender.

5 PROJECT PLANNING AND CONTROL: A critical path analysis (CPA) comprising 75 activities was used to plan both pre-construction and construction phases. The programme was monitored monthly but never updated. There were few reports, but meetings were held at least weekly throughout the project in Japan, San Francisco or Atlanta; the client's representative was heavily involved in all these meetings.

6 DESIGN AND CONSTRUCTION SOLUTION: The building was an orthodox single storey, steel frame, metal sheet clad industrial unit, with a small air-conditioned, office section. The structure blended with the surrounding buildings and provided for easy extension of the manufacturing element without disrupting production. Banks of earth to cill height on the southern and western perimeters of the building reduced solar gain. It was a greenfield site.

7 ASSESSMENT: All parties seemed pleased with the outcome. The building was completed by the tight deadline and, as a result, the client started production on the day specified the previous year. In doing so, he paid acceleration costs to cover the late changes in design proposed from within his own organisation. Although there were several problems, including the need to change the external cladding because of difficulties in the supply of the materials originally specified, it was felt that these were readily overcome. Several factors were identified as significant in enabling the achievement of the deadline. These were:
   a. the simplicity of the original design;
   b. the phasing of design and construction;
   c. the flexibility of the contractual arrangement which enabled the introduction of late changes in design at low cost;
   d. the desire of the consultants and contractor to perform well for a large and potentially important client.

CASE DESCRIPTION   US3

OFFICES   UTAH $29m   33 months

1   TYPE OF CLIENT: Public utility company, secondary constructor, experienced.

2   CLIENT REQUIREMENTS: At a time when leases were running out and a new retail outlet was required, this client wanted to bring together all its offices in one location. The chosen site was situated in an urban area across the road from the company's computer installation. The client had a well defined requirement for a particular completion date but the main project constraint was a very tight budget.

3.   CONTRACTUAL APPROACH: although experienced in construction, the client had not previously commissioned the building of such a major facility. He was advised to adopt construction management because it would provide him, from the beginning of the design period, with the expertise necessary to ensure that he would get a building which he could afford. The non-negotiable budget generated a number of value engineering exercises which reduced the cost of the building from $38m to $29m. The contract also allowed the client to phase design with construction and take advantage of changing market conditions, as prices fell during the project period.

4   CLIENT TEAM: Internally, the client had a full time project manager, who was an architect by training and had worked in that position for a long time. having established the requirements of the company's various departments, the clients representative had the executive powers and seniority to make decisions quickly.
The client appointed a local firm of architects but, because of the size of the project, he interviewed a number of 'out of state' professional construction managers. The construction managers appointed were directly responsible to the client for progress and cost. The architect appointed his own engineering consultants and the full project team, consisting of architect, construction manager and client was established early in the project.

5   PROJECT PLANNING AND CONTROL: The project team on the case used the most rigorous systems encountered in the study. A critical path analysis, comprising 132 activities was used to plan and control the entire project. During construction, the programme was monitored monthly and updated on four occasions. From the CPA bar charts were derived for trades and areas.
There were weekly meetings at all stages and formal weekly reports were a significant feature of the methods of control.

6   DESIGN AND CONSTRUCTION SOLUTION: because of the tight budget limits, a number of value engineering exercises were undertaken. Through these, the client's space requirements were calculated to be less than his original estimates and this revision allowed 4 floors to be taken off the office block. Similarly, the provision of a coach service from suburban locations reduced the number of car parking spaces necessary in the multi storey car park.
A 16 storey steel frame with metal deck and concrete floors was chosen for its speed, simplicity and marginal cost saving. In order to reduce energy consumption, heat exhausted from the existing computer block on the opposite side of the road was used to augment the heating of the new building.

7   ASSESSMENT: The client was particularly pleased with the outcome, since he actually moved into his building on time and paid no more than he had budgeted for, even though this was

considerably below the original estimates. He felt that his decision to use construction management was vindicated. This is because it allowed him to consider the cost implications of decision throughout the project and because it provided the flexibility required to implement changes without undue difficulty. For example, mid-way through construction, it became apparent that the difference between actual internally generated cash and construction loan interest was beyond that predicted and that this would lead to corporate cash limits being exceeded. Since the final bid packages had not yet been let, their sequence and construction periods were amended so that areas of the office block would be finished ahead of time to take in staff and open the retail area early.

Several factors contributed to the achievement of the client's objectives. These were:

a. the flexibility provided by the contractual arrangement;
b. the high degree of project management;
c. the relative simplicity and standardisation of the design;
d. the high degree of co-operation within the professional team led by the construction manager.

CASE DESCRIPTION   US4

WAREHOUSE   CALIFORNIA $35m   23 months

1   TYPE OF CLIENT: Private supermarket chain, secondary constructor, not experienced.

2   CLIENT REQUIREMENTS: The company wanted a distribution centre to serve its supermarkets in Northern California. A large proportion of the warehouse was to be devoted to cold stores and the rest was to be racked out. These two items together determined the size and configuration of the building.

As the equipment was the major factor in the cost of the total development, the actual cost of the building was secondary. More important was the date for completion so that distribution could begin in time for the Christmas season.

3   CONTRACTUAL APPROACH: The architect, who had worked with the client before, recommended a construction management approach, because of the short project period and the need to overlap the design and construction phases in order to achieve the completion date. This was also seen as the only way to ensure adequate coordination between the equipment manufacturer's changing requirements and the design of the shell.

4   CLIENT TEAM: The client, who had a limited experience of commissioning new facilities, had three different representatives responsible for the project during its progress. These representatives were senior managers who, in addition to this project responsibility, had a heavy work load within the organisation. These arrangements resulted in time pressures and produced certain problems of continuity but were counterbalanced by the managers' seniority and power to make decisions quickly.

The client chose an architect who had worked for him before and who specialised in buildings for the food industry. This practice also employed civil and structural engineers, but contracted out other specialist engineering functions. The construction manager was the only other member of the team who was directly appointed by the client on the recommendation of the architect. The construction manager was responsible for progress and cost. These team members had worked together before and reported good working relationships.

5   PROJECT PLANNING AND CONTROL: At the preconstruction stage a linked bar chart comprising 25 activities was used. At the construction stage a critical path analysis comprising 70 activities was used. This programme was monitored monthly but never updated. The CPA was converted into hand drawn bar chart form to ease communication. There were regular monthly meetings and formal reports.

6   DESIGN AND CONSTRUCTION SOLUTION: The design was determined by the layout defined by the equipment suppliers. The simplest and most economical building was judged to be a steel frame clad with concrete tilt-up panels. The tolerances demanded by the equipment supplier were initially thought to be too tight and discussion with him produced several changes, including a larger floor tolerance. This in turn led to a lower cost for the structural floor.

7   ASSESSMENT: The client was pleased to obtain his distribution centre on time and below budget. He did so by using a large number of local contractors and felt that this helped his image in the community. The factors identified as contributing to the success of the project were:

    a.   the contractual approach which encouraged a flexible approach to the achievement of a tight time scale;
    b.   the good relationships between members of the project team who had worked together before and seemed to communicate easily.

CASE DESCRIPTION   US5

FACTORY   CALIFORNIA $22m   8 months

1   TYPE OF CLIENT: Subsidiary of major Japanese vehicle manufacturer, secondary constructor, inexperienced in USA.

2   CLIENT REQUIREMENTS: The client wanted to double his production of truck beds within twelve months of appointing the team. This had to be achieved by extending his existing factory and introducing new process equipment (e.g. paint spraying) whilst maintaining full production. The new equipment was to be installed in the summer shutdown and to be completed ready for production when the operatives returned. Time was of the essence.

3   CONTRACTUAL APPROACH: The client chose a design-build contract for two main reasons. First, the total time available for the design and construction was extremely limited. (11 months) Second, it was recognised that since the Japanese style of management demanded consensus within the organisation, decision making was likely to be a lengthy process. Hence the external communication paths needed to be very short and simple. Having decided to work on a design build basis, the particular firm was chosen for its local knowledge, experience and reputation.

4   CLIENT TEAM: the client appointed as his internal representative an American manager who was experienced in project managing new facilities. At the majority of design meetings, he was supported by two or three Japanese engineers and the same number of American engineers. There was also a substantial input from engineers in Japan.
    The design-build contractor had a lead co-ordinator, an architect by training, who attended all the meetings and acted as the primary contact for the company. He was responsible for linking the other design and construction disciplines within his own organisation.

5 PROJECT PLANNING AND CONTROL: A bar chart was used to plan all stages of the project. During the early stages of construction the programme was monitored monthly, increasing to fortnightly at the final stages. Due to the changing requirements of the many concerned parties, the programme was updated nine times.
For the same reason there were numerous meetings and reports throughout the project.

6 DESIGN AND CONSTRUCTION SOLUTION: The building structure, finishes and services were determined by the need to match the existing building in order to satisfy the local planning laws, which were very onerous. The other major design decisions were the result of discussions between the internal process engineers and the equipment sub-contractors. The building envelope was a steel frame clad with metal sheets.

7 ASSESSMENT: The extended factory started producing the required number of additional truck beds on the predicted date. The client thus achieved his objective, admittedly at some cost in overtime payments, due to changes and late decisions. However, overall he was delighted and has given the design-build contractor another contract as a result.
The important influences on this project were described as:

a. the simplicity and flexibility afforded by the design build contract.
b. the expertise and experience of the design-build contractor.
c. the ability of the client to incur additional costs in the interests of speed of construction.

CASE DESCRIPTION   US6

OFFICES   MASSACHUSETTS $14.4m   16 months

1 TYPE OF CLIENT: Privately owned property developer, primary constructor, experienced.

2 CLIENT REQUIREMENTS: A well designed, well built office block constructed for a known price, within the total budget and ready for some tenants who had already signed leases.

3 CONTRACTUAL APPROACH: The client negotiated a Guaranteed Maximum Price with bonus and liquidated damages clauses with a contractor he had used before and who had an outstanding reputation for quality. Because he wished to retain the completed buildings within his port-folio, the client insisted on a high quality product. Having used this contractual arrangement before, he was confident it would achieve this objective with a known contractor.

4 CLIENT TEAM: The client was represented on a regular basis by two people. The first was the construction manager, who had previously been employed by the contractors, and who had day to day responsibility for the project. The second was the vice-president who had extensive experience in managing construction and property and who had direct responsibility to the board for the profitability of the project. Both of them attended all design meetings and the main site meetings.
The architectural firm was chosen because of its known design skills and its ability to get on with the city authorities who were judging the competition for the site from submissions from a number of developers. The consulting engineers were chosen by and worked for the architect. The contractor was chosen early by the client and attended design meetings, giving cost and construction advice.

5   PROJECT PLANNING AND CONTROL: At the preconstruction stage there was no formal programme. At the construction stage a bar chart comprising 30 activities was used. Monitoring was carried out monthly but there was no updating. Meetings were held fortnightly during construction. Formal reporting however was rarely used.

6   DESIGN AND CONSTRUCTION SOLUTION: The architects won the competition because the function, scale and appearance of their proposal related best to the surrounding area. The brick clad exterior blended easily with the adjacent buildings. The interior was standard for US office buildings, where only services, toilets on each floor and the suspended ceiling grid was provided by the developer. Any partitioning, floor, wall and ceiling finishes would be provided by the tenant. A simple standard bay, flat slab, reinforced concrete frame structure was chosen for speed and economy.

7   ASSESSMENT: The project was clearly successful in that the client achieved his objectives of quality, cost and time. The architect was pleased with the result and the contractor was also delighted, being awarded a bonus for early completion.
    The ingredients of the project's success were identified as:

    a.   the characteristics of the client who was experienced, had a clear knowledge of his require-ments and the ability to make decisions quickly; in addition, his construction manager was familiar with the approach and systems of the contractor;
    b.   the contractual arrangement, which allowed a flexible approach;
    c.   the efficiency of the architect who worked closely with the contractor from the early stages to completion. The relationship between the design team and contractor was reported to be very good, with regular meetings being supplemented by frequent discussions on the phone.
    d.   the high quality which was achieved was within the specified, but not unduly restrictive budget.

CASE DESCRIPTION   UK1

OFFICES   LONDON   £8.7m   31 months

1   TYPE OF CLIENT: Property developer, primary constructor, experienced.

2   CLIENT REQUIREMENTS: This major property developer wanted a high quality shop and office development to meet the many planning and statutory control requirements of a sensitive central urban environment.

3   CONTRACTUAL APPROACH: The client decided to adopt a two stage negotiated contract with the contractor who was already on site constructing the first phase for a different client.

4   CLIENT TEAM: Internally the client had a project manager, experienced in construction, who had full time responsibility for a number of projects. In addition, one of the directors attended both the major design and construction meetings.
    The design team comprised the architect, consulting engineers and quantity surveyor. Each of these consultants is pre-eminent in his field and is known for his expertise in handling complex urban developments. There was also a clerk of works appointed by the client.

5   PROJECT PLANNING AND CONTROL: Milestone dates were used to plan the preconstruc-tion stage. During construction a bar chart comprising 101 activities was used. This programme

was monitored monthly. Meetings were held and reports made on a monthly basis during construction.

6 DESIGN AND CONSTRUCTION SOLUTION: The design which was eventually adopted was one which had to satisfy five different statutory authorities. The design solution also had to be acceptable to the Royal Fine Arts Commission, whilst at the same time meeting the engineering requirements demanded by the London Transport Executive whose underground station was directly beneath the development.

The design was also influenced by the location of the building which occupied a corner site. Thus, in addition to serving two functions, shopping and office development, the structure had to blend with different existing facades. To meet these demands, the designers adopted brick and curtain walling exteriors. Structurally, the engineers were compelled to adopt a reinforced concrete transfer structure above the underground station and the customary dropped beam around the suspended floor slabs in order to comply with floor to ceiling levels established by the adjacent buildings.

7 ASSESSMENT: The numerous constraints already described limited both the design solution and the contractual arrangement, leaving the client and design team scant scope for other alternatives.

The complexity of the planning problems, and the requirement for a high level of quality of design and construction, combined to make this a relatively high cost, low speed project.

CASE DESCRIPTION   UK2

OFFICES   BUCKINGHAMSHIRE   £2.5m   18 months

1 TYPE OF CLIENT: Property developer, primary constructor, experienced.

2 CLIENT REQUIREMENTS: The client wanted a speculative office development to be built to meet an overall specification set by the local authority. He had a well defined and tight time schedule.

3 CONTRACTUAL APPROACH: In order to be assured of achieving the tight design and construction period, a contract was negotiated with a contractor who had performed well for the client on previous occasions.

4 CLIENT TEAM: The client appointed an experienced and knowledgeable external project manager to represent him at meetings and liaise with the design and construction teams.

The design team comprised the architect, quantity surveyor, engineers, and contractor, who was responsible for the programming aspects of construction. There was also a clerk of works appointed by the client. The offices of the architect and quantity surveyor were on the same floor in the same building. The contractor was also located nearby.

5 PROJECT PLANNING AND CONTROL: Milestone dates were used to plan the preconstruction stage. During construction a bar chart comprising 62 activities was used. This programme was monitored monthly.

During construction, meetings were held and reports made on a monthly basis.

6   DESIGN AND CONSTRUCTION SOLUTION: The design adopted was a standard brick clad, reinforced concrete framed office block, which blended with the others in the vicinity and conformed to the other criteria stated by the development corporation. There were no internal partitions, but lobbies, toilets and services were installed throughout.

7   ASSESSMENT: Those involved were generally pleased with the project and the fact that the building was finished on time and within budget. The factors influencing project performance included:

   a.   the origins of the project. It was the architect who originally identified the need for the office block, liaised, with the local authority, contacted a property developer and put the package together. Without this initiative, the client concerned would not have developed the particular building. This common interest and early involvement may be one of the reasons why the working relationships between the client, consultants and contractor were generally considered to be good.
   b.   the contractual arrangements, which appeared to work well.
   c.   the phyicical proximity of the major parties, which eased communication.

CASE DESCRIPTION   UK3

OFFICES   HAMPSHIRE   £8.2m   18 months

1   TYPE OF CLIENT: Manufacturing subsidiary of major multi-national, secondary constructor, experienced.

2   CLIENT REQUIREMENTS: the client required a building of exceptional quality, equal to its current corporate offices on the adjacent site. The new office building was to provide 139,000 square feet gross area, 112,000 square feet net area and parking for 400 cars. It was to be designed such that it could be occupied either by the client or let in the open market. There was a tight time deadline and fixed budget, thus making this the only project in the UK sample for which clients had demanding requirements on cost, time and quality.

3   CONTRACTUAL APPROACH: The client chose a management contract for several reasons. First, the need for a relatively short project period demanded an early start on site. Second, the clients and consultants already had successful experience with this contractual arrangement in building their previous corporate offices. Third, the consultants wanted the maximum competition and recommended the management form of contract.

4.   CLIENT TEAM: In the early stages of the project, the client had an in-house architect as client representative. However, for the major part the company secretary liaised with the consultants, who were a multi-disciplinary team encompassing all the skills which were needed.

5   PROJECT PLANNING AND CONTROL: Bar charts were used to plan the whole project. The programme for the construction phase comprised 91 activities and was monitored monthly.
There were weekly meetings within the multi-disciplinary design group throughout the project.

6   DESIGN AND CONSTRUCTION SOLUTION: The design of the offices resulted from consideration of three factors: their relationship to the adjacent building in terms of siting, massing and quality; efficiency of internal planning and, finally, economy of construction and running costs.

The building has a high quality specification and will be economical to run, being naturally ventilated and heated by radiators, each fitted with a thermostatic valve. In summer the five foot deep overhangs all round the outside elevations will ensure that solar gain is kept to a minimum. Electrical and telephone services run in the floor to give maximum flexibility, and light fittings are integrated into the design of the structural ceiling. Practically all of the horizontal structure is precast concrete, ensuring speed of erection, dry construction and high quality finish.

7 ASSESSMENT: All those involved regard this as a successful project and identified the following as ingredients of that success:

   a. the client had a clear idea of what he wanted and did not change his mind; the design was frozen before any tendering;
   b. the design team who had worked with the client before, on the adjacent site knew how to translate those ideas into practice vary rapidly;
   c. the design team who had also worked together on many projects before, and being located in the same large studio were able to communicate readily with each other;
   d. the members of the design team were very aware of the contractual and constructional factors which lead to high quality, speedy and relatively low cost buildings, and incorporated those ideas into the project.

CASE DESCRIPTION   UK4

OFFICES   LONDON   £10.9m   25 months

1 TYPE OF CLIENT: Subsidiary of major private multi-national engineering company, secondary constructor, experienced.

2 CLIENT REQUIREMENTS: An extension to accommodate more staff and to match the existing office block, 220,000 square feet gross and 165,000 square feet net. The quality was thus determined by the existing building. A strict budget was set and maintained.

3 CONTRACTUAL APPROACH: A two stage tender with approximate bills, and open competition on the major sub-trades was adopted. Six contractors bid on approximate bills and a submission and interview. The lowest bidder was not awarded the contract. The contractor with the most convincing staff and ideas were selected.

4 CLIENT TEAM: Internally, the client had an experienced construction manager who exercised a full-time controlling brief to translate the internal requirements into the project. During the construction phase there was an additional full-time assistant project manager. As this was to be an extension, the design team which successfully carried out the previous office block were used. This comprised an architect, consulting structural engineer and quantity surveyor. The engineering services were part of a design/build package, which was watched over by a consulting engineer.

5 DESIGN SOLUTION: The design resulted from the requirement to relate to the existing building in both its external treatment and internal planning. In addition the increasing traffic noise demanded double glazing and hence air-conditioning. The curtain walling adopted matched the existing and the structure was similarly limited to a reinforced concrete frame with suspended slabs having a dropped edge beam.

6 PROJECT PLANNING AND CONTROL: Milestone dates were used at the pre-construction stage. A bar chart was used during construction and monitored monthly. Meetings at which reports were presented were held on a monthly basis.

7 ASSESSMENT: The client achieved his objectives of quality, cost and the building was finished on time. In relation to the rest of the UK sample, it was erected fastest and at low cost. The client felt that the contractual arrangement gave the advantages of a management contract in that there was maximum competition on each of the trades, whilst retaining the comfort of a tendered maximum price, which was negotiated in a less adversarial manner.

Acknowledgements
We would like to thank all those people who gave of their time and knowledge to discuss particular projects. They were drawn from the following organisations:

APC International	Roger Hobbs, John Corby & Associates
Arup Associates	Holder Construction Company
Ove Arup and Partners	Kaiser Engineering
Austin Company	Matthew Hall Mechanical Services
The Beacon Companies	Maxell America Inc.
Blount Brothers Corporation	MEPC Plc
Edward Bonelli and Associates	Mountain Bell
Boston Properties	Skidmore, Owings & Merill
Chapman Taylor Partners	Southern Central Bell
C M Inc.	Cyril Sweett & Partners
Henry Cooper & Sons	Sydney Kaye Firmin Partnership
Davis & Brodie Associates	Toyota Motor Manufacturing
John Deere Corporation	Turner Construction Company
Giattina and Associates	United Grocers Ltd
Gulf Oil Corporation	Wiggins Teape Plc
Haden Young	Winter Company Builders Inc
Heery Associates	Zukas Magasiner Green

We would also like to thank those individuals who gave their time and experience to discuss the general topics examined in the report. They included:

Donald Barrie, Kaiser Engineers
Professor J. Becker, Massachussets Institute of Technology
Ron Clarke, Cyril Sweett & Partners
Mike Davies, Richard Rogers & Partners
Terry Fleming, Laing Management Contracting
Professor Fondahl, Stanford University
George Heery, Heery & Heery
Bob Hobbs, Arup Associates
Professor H. Irwig, Massachussets Institute of Technology
Professor R. Leavitt, Stanford University
John Pilkington, Ove Arup & Partners
David Thomas, C M Inc.
Norman Wakefield, Y J Lovell (Holdings)

Finally, we would like to thank Jane Thompson for her patience and forebearance in typing and editing the many 'final' drafts of this report!